A Guide to Ancient Maya Ruins

Second Edition, Revised and Enlarged

A Guide to Ancient Maya Ruins

By C. Bruce Hunter

University of Oklahoma Press : Norman and London

By C. Bruce Hunter

A Guide to Ancient Maya Ruins (Norman, 1974; revised edition, 1986)
A Guide to Ancient Mexican Ruins (Norman, 1977)

Library of Congress Cataloging-in-Publication Data

Hunter, C. Bruce.
  A guide to ancient Maya ruins.

  Bibliography: p. 331
  Includes index.
    1. Mayas—Antiquities.   2. Mexico—Antiquities.
  3. Central America—Antiquities.   I. Title.
  F1435.H86   1986   972'.01   85–22586
  ISBN 0–8061–1973–X (cloth)
  ISBN 0–8061–1992–6 (paper)

2   3   4   5   6   7   8   9   10   11   12   13   14   15   16   17   18   19   20

For

Manuel Dominguez

Victor Rendon

Contents

Illustrations

Color Plates (following page 146)

Black-and-White Illustrations

Maps and Site Plans

Preface to the Second Edition

In the thirty years that I have been leading field-study trips to Maya archaeological zones for the American Museum of Natural History, I have seen the number of travelers to these areas increase tremendously. During this time the need for an adequate guide to the accessible ruins and to the means of getting to them has become apparent. This book is written for the traveler who wishes to explore some of the great Maya ceremonial centers. Thus the sites included here are those that can be reached without great difficulty, even though some are in remote regions.

Since the first edition of *A Guide to Ancient Maya Ruins* was published in 1974, much new material on the Maya has become available. Recent research has thrown new light on the very beginning as well as the collapse of the Maya civilization, the importance of the ruling dynasties and marriage alliances between great ruling families, the relevance of trade routes and trade centers, and the political and social interaction between the larger "city-states" and their outlying towns and villages. In the past few years excavations at Palenque, Quiriguá, Edzna, Cobá, and many other sites have reawakened interest in how ancient Maya cities may have functioned.

In this revision some material is entirely new. The sections on Cobá and Edzna have been added, along with new information on the structures at other archaeological zones. Although some sections of the book have been left intact, others have been changed because of recent findings. New excavations at such sites as Cuello, in Belize, and Abaj Takalik, in Guatemala, have altered our thinking about the development of the Maya civilization. Also, a better understanding of the Maya writing system has made it possible to piece together more of the historical data recorded on Maya monuments.

A Guide to Ancient Maya Ruins

For more than a century and a quarter the magnificent ruins of the Maya civilization in the jungles and highlands of Mesoamerica have excited the imagination and curiosity of people all over the world. At one time only the most intrepid of explorers and scientists, traveling by muleback or on foot and hacking their way through the jungle with machetes, could see for themselves the remnants of what was once a great civilization. Today, however, with the construction of roads, bridges, and airfields, a number of important and impressive sites are open to tourists.

Descriptions, explanations, analyses, and appraisals of the Maya cities with their elaborate ceremonial centers, structures, and sculptures are now readily available. Today, far from being mysterious and forbidding monuments, as they seemed to their discoverers, these Maya cities assume their proper importance in history and rank with other great civilizations throughout the world.

This book is primarily for the traveler. Regardless of their importance, therefore, I have not included some Maya centers, such as Uaxactún, Piedras Negras, and Altar de Sacrificios and many other ruins in the Petén and Río Bec areas. These either have not been restored or are still extremely difficult to reach.

If *A Guide to Ancient Maya Ruins* can help travelers decide which archaeological zones to visit, and if it can make the trip more enjoyable and what they see more comprehensible, then my purpose in writing it has been accomplished.

The revision of this guide could not have been possible without the aid of many people engaged in Maya research and others who have given technical and editorial assistance. To these people I extend my sincere appreciation.

Fort Salonga, New York   C. Bruce Hunter

A Guide to Ancient Maya Ruins

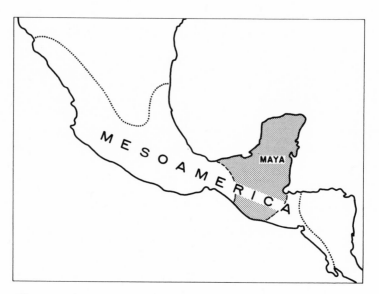

The approximate extent of Mesoamerica.

1   Introduction

The first movement of peoples from the Asiatic mainland to the Americas, their mode of transportation, and their reason for leaving their homeland are still something of a mystery. A northern land bridge between the two continents made it possible for easy immigration between 25,000 and 9000 B.C. (the land bridge disappeared when the sea rose during the Wisconsin deglaciation). There is a belief among some archaeologists, however, that man may have reached the North American continent at a much earlier time, possibly as early as 50,000 to 100,000 B.C. In any case, the movement of peoples along the coastal waters and overland into the Americas was rapid. By 10,000 B.C. these migrating peoples, organized into small hunting and fishing bands, had populated the Americas all the way south to Tierra del Fuego. They became the first "native Americans."

Sometime between 5000 and 2000 B.C. (the Archaic Period) the domestication of fruits and vegetables was begun, and many of the hunting and fishing groups settled into a more sedentary life in hamlets, with agriculture the basis of the economy. By 1500 B.C. (the Early Preclassic Period) the Maya region was well populated, as were many other regions in Mesoamerica.

The first two major civilizations to emerge in the Americas were on two separate continents. In South America during the Middle Preclassic Period (1200-400 B.C.) a dominant culture developed in Peru, now known as Chavín. Remains of the stone structures from this time are still visible today at what is believed to have been its capital, Chavín de Huantar. In Mesoamerica the culture contemporary to Chavín was that of the Olmec, in the coastal region of Veracruz. Both civilizations had well-developed economic and religious institutions, and authority was vested in hereditary chiefs. Both civilizations also had a tremendous effect on other developing cultures in far-flung areas of Mesoamerica and South America. When these two important cultures came to an end, the Maya had already settled in communities along the Pacific Slope as well as other areas, and many other cultures were on the ascendancy on both continents.

As early as 2500 B.C. the Maya were already established in village areas and involved in trade and ceremonials. That era was before the Greeks or Romans had created their great civilizations and before the Shang Dynasty in China had produced the masterful bronze altarpieces that have awed the Western world ever since. Recent archaeological investigations by Norman Hammond at Cuello, in northern Belize, give us some indication of household objects of daily use (such as the metate, mano, and pottery), and trade items during this third millennium B.C. These early Maya beginnings preceded the Olmec florescence by a thousand years. The Maya civilization, however, evolved with a slow, steady growth that was not to reach its peak until the Late Classic Period (A.D. 600-900).

Buildings became more numerous and more elaborate during the Early and Middle Preclassic periods. Several sites from the Middle Preclassic Period (1200-400 B.C.) show constant occupation by the Maya as early as 900 B.C. To name a few, there are Becan, in southeastern Campeche near Belize; Cuello, in northern Belize; Tikal, in the Petén; Seibal and Altar de Sacrificios, on the Río Pasión; and Dzibilchaltún and Edzná, in the Northern Lowlands. At some of these sites there is evidence of home industries, town planning, trade with distant areas, bark beating (possibly to make writing materials), and there is indication of a stratified social structure, ceremonials, and the importance of ancestral worship, which was to be the obsession of the Maya elite for the next 1,500 years. At Becan there is evidence of extensive fortifications in Late Preclassic times, dispelling the theory of the "peaceful" Maya. There is indication of fortifications at Tikal a little later. A cooperative laboring class must have been available to build such fortifications, as well as the ceremonial platforms, pyramids, palace structures, and administrative buildings for the elite of Maya society of that time. No doubt the labor of slaves captured in battle was also utilized.

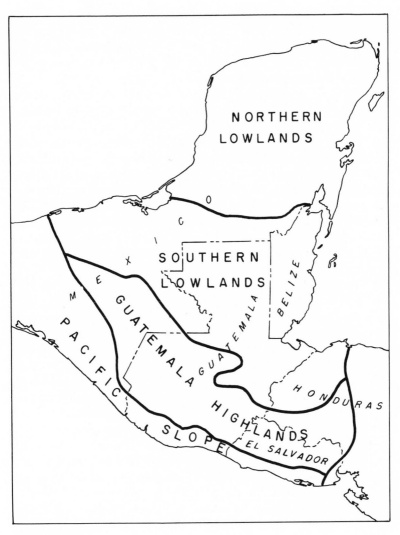

The Maya area.

Maya ceremonial centers.

Between 600 B.C. and A.D. 250 great activity in city planning was taking place all over Mesoamerica. Cultural areas were defined. Ceremonial complexes in the heart of the cities were constructed, and trade routes and luxury goods fostered trade competition between regions. Mathematics, astronomy, and writing were the concerns of academicians of the time. The calendar was well established in Late Preclassic times, and we see the earliest of the Long Count dates on Stela 2 at Chiapa de Corzo (36 B.C.), Tres Zapotes on Stela C (31 B.C.), and Stela 1 at El Baúl (A.D. 31).[1] In Late Preclassic times the most important city in the Northern Lowlands was Dzibilchaltún; in the Southern Lowlands, El Mirador; and in the Highlands, Kaminaljuyú.

As the Maya civilization emerged, it did not do so in total isolation from other cultural groups. In fact, throughout their history they felt the influence of other cultures, such as the Olmec and Izapa in Late Preclassic times, Teotihuacán and El Tajín in Classic times, and the Toltec and Aztec in the Postclassic Period in Yucatán and the Guatemala Highlands. Naturally, the Maya also influenced other Classic civilizations in Mesoamerica. Their complex ceremonials, elaborate court etiquette, cosmology, calendrics, and mathematics did not go unnoticed by other civilizations of the era. Recent excavations at Cacaxtla, Mexico, far from the Maya heartland, have revealed well-preserved murals showing the tremendous influence of the Maya.

During the Classic Period, which started as early as A.D. 250 in some areas and ended as late as A.D. 900 in others, Mesoamerica reached a florescence in cultural development that was never to be equaled. In northern Mesoamerica the greatest of the Classic civilizations was Teotihuacán. Its capital site, approximately thirty miles north of present-day Mexico City, had a population somewhere between 75,000 and 125,000 persons—a population much larger than that of most European cities of that time. The influence of Teotihuacán was felt throughout all of Mesoamerica. Its people built a second major city at Kaminaljuyú and controlled trade routes

---

[1]For an explanation of the Long Count, see chapter 10.

7

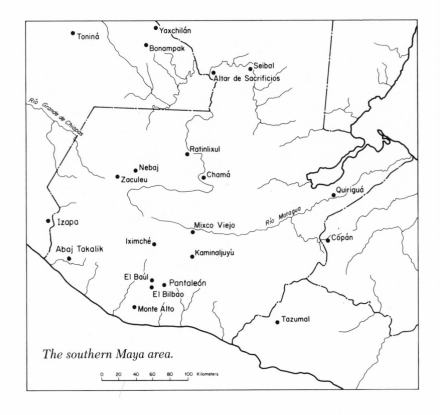

The southern Maya area.

0   20   40   60   80   100 Kilometers

throughout a large part of Mesoamerica. Other important cultural areas during the Classic Period were the Cholula region, Classic Veracruz, and Monte Albán. The last had been under the control of the Zapotecs from Preclassic times and their language and culture still persist in the region today. At the southern end of Mesoamerica during Classic times the Maya dominated the southern part of present-day Mexico, including the Yucatán Peninsula and all of Guatemala, Honduras, Belize, and El Salvador. Their influence was extraordinary, affecting cultures from Costa Rica to the Mexican highlands.

During this same period Europe was well entrenched in the Dark Ages and knew little of the rest of the world; India and

China were in their "Golden Age," with the ascendancy of the Gupta and T'ang dynasties, respectively, while the Maya were blossoming into the greatest of all civilizations in the New World. Maya scientists had accomplished feats in astronomy and mathematics not equaled by their contemporaries in the Old World. Accomplishments in the arts had reached a sophistication comparable to that of any other great traditional culture anywhere.

At the ceremonial center of Palenque delicate stucco reliefs decorated the magnificent façades of temple and palace buildings. Tikal architects designed and constructed the tallest of all pyramid temples in the heart of the Petén jungle. Copán was the most southerly of the larger Maya cities, and the scientists there startled their contemporaries with their developments in astronomy and hieroglyphic writing, both of which they recorded on carved stone monuments and in books that have since perished. Architects at ceremonial centers in the Puuc Hills of Northern Yucatán created masterpieces in stone mosaic as decorations for their splendid "palaces," as well as on other types of structures. Wall paintings, some in true fresco style, adorned the temples and other structures throughout the land, creating a brilliance in the tropical sun that could only astound those persons paying homage at the ceremonial centers. The glowing colors of the frescoes at Bonampak, now over a thousand years old, hint at the excellence of art throughout the Maya civilization. As we look at the somber stone structures in the Maya area today, it is hard to imagine that these buildings were once completely painted in brilliant colors in much the same way that Greek temples were painted during the Greeks' Golden Age. The Maya were lavish with red for the ceremonial buildings. Some of the other colors used were greens, blues, and yellows. The monuments that studded the large ceremonial plazas were also painted.

As mentioned earlier, Maya territory extended from El Salvador and Honduras into Guatemala and Belize, north to the Yucatán Peninsula, and west as far as Tabasco and Chiapas. It would seem that the territory was divided into large city-states, controlled by ruling families who may have been both political and religious leaders of their realm. The extent and exact nature of these po-

Hieroglyphic Recordings of a Few Events
During Classic Maya History

Year (A.D.)	Event
279	Earliest known Lowland Maya dynastic monument displaying Tikal's emblem glyph, Stela 29
317	Probable portrait of Tikal's first ruler, Jaguar Paw, Leyden Plate
376	Curl Nose portrayed, Stela 4, Tikal
416	Accession of Stormy Sky at Tikal
455	Possible date of earliest ruler at Quiriguá, Monument 3, (erected A.D. 775)
455	Death of Stormy Sky, Tikal, Burial 48
475	Accession of Kan Boar at Tikal
	Accession of Jaguar Paw Skull at Tikal
514	Earliest known Yaxchilán emblem glyph, Stela 27
534	Earliest known Piedras Negras emblem glyph, Lintel 12
	Accession of Double Bird at Tikal, Stela 17
554	Earliest known Copán emblem glyph, Stela 9
593	Earliest known Palenque emblem glyph, Hieroglyphic Stairway
613	Accession of Lord Pacal at Palenque
633	Accession of Bird Jaguar at Yaxchilán (approximate date)
672	Accession of Ah Cacau at Tikal, Temple I lintel
	Accession of Shield Jaguar at Yaxchilán
683	Death of Lord Pacal, Palenque, Temple of the Inscriptions
	Accession of Chan Bahlum at Palenque
692	Death of Chan Bahlum
	Accession of Kan Xul at Palenque
711	Accession of Chaacal at Palenque
	Accession of Chac Zutz at Palenque
	Accession of Cauac Sky at Quiriguá, Monument 10
731	Earliest known Quiriguá emblem glyph
	Emblem glyphs of Palenque, Tikal, Copán, and (?)Calakmul
	Accession of Yax Kin at Tikal, Stela 21
	Cauac Sky, ruler of Quiriguá, captures Eighteen Rabbit, ruler of Copán
	Accession of Bird Jaguar III at Yaxchilán
751	Earliest known Seibal emblem glyph, South Hieroglyphic Stairway

	Accession of Sun-at-Horizon at Copán
	Accession of Lord Kuk at Palenque
	Accession of Chitam at Tikal, Stela 22
771	Accession of Yax Sky at Copán, Altar F
	Accession of Sky Xul at Quiriguá, Monument 7
790	Accession of Six Cimi at Palenque
	Accession of Jade Sky at Quiriguá
909	The latest known date recorded in the Southern Lowlands, Tonina, Monument 101

litical areas is unknown. Recent research on Maya hieroglyphic writing gives us some historical information about the ruling dynasties of a number of Maya cities (see the following table). The hieroglyphics also describe marriage alliances linking these elite families with those of other city-states. Such marriages helped establish political alliances, the geographic boundaries of the rulers' domains, and a homogeneity in the arts and sciences.

The ruling elite organized the social structure of the city-states and all the attendant activities. Dedicatory statues in the form of stelae stand at many ceremonial centers, and research by Tatiana Proskouriakoff on genealogies of Maya monuments suggests that the rulers may have been considered to have divine power. The Maya civilization, apparently coexisting in relative peace with neighboring cultures, matured for approximately fifteen hundred years, developing in the arts and sciences with few major interruptions. After reaching a Classic florescence that lasted some six hundred years (A.D. 300–900), the civilization began to decline. Many cities were abandoned, the arts deteriorated rapidly, and foreign control or influence was apparent. In the Guatemala Highlands the Maya shifted their cities and towns to hilltop locations that could be fortified. With the arrival of the Spaniards, however, it was obvious that the Maya would never rise again as a world civilization.

For many years writers sought ways to explain the "great mystery" of the Maya "collapse" at the end of the Late Classic Period. According to modern scholars, the traditional term "collapse" now clearly seems inappropriate. Rather than suddenly falling

11

apart, the Classic Maya experienced internal and external changes that led to a "cultural decline."

All civilizations apparently must go through the cycle of beginning, flowering, and ending, and the Maya were no exception, although they enjoyed an unusually long civilization in comparison to the cycles of other cultures in the New World. The Inca, Toltec, and Aztec lasted fewer than five hundred years each. One of the many writers who have offered explanations for the Maya downfall, Sir J. Eric S. Thompson, has given us in *Maya History and Religion* a plausible explanation. In brief, during Late Classic times the Maya political and religious system began to erode, in some places as early as three hundred years before the Maya decline. Local cult deities and household gods gained appeal as opposed to the pantheon of gods worshiped at the large ceremonial centers by the old priestly and ruling classes. Also, the hamlets administered by local rulers pressed for more autonomy as their communities grew into larger towns and cities. The work required to construct the great ceremonial centers was a tremendous drain on the energy of the laboring class of people in the hamlets. Feeding the large populations in the Maya cities became a burdensome problem during Late Classic times. The Maya tried to solve this problem by shifting some land areas to more intensive agricultural development. In many areas terraced fields were constructed. Extensive use was made of swamps and other wetland areas by establishing raised fields. Canals and reservoirs were constructed to control water levels. Other land areas were shifted from swidden (slash-and-burn) agriculture to orchards of food-producing crops such as ramon, breadnut, cacao, sapodilla, and avocado. Even with these efforts, as recent research indicates, endemic diseases and malnutrition were common in some areas. The problem was further complicated by a widespread drought that began in A.D. 850.

The delicate balance within the Maya social system could not withstand the disparity between an overworked laboring class and an overbearing ruling and priestly class. Revolt or abandonment of the entire area was inevitable. Just when the Maya ruling chiefs were having problems with their own cities, groups of militant people from the Valley of Mexico and the Gulf states were pushing deeper into the Maya area, disrupting extremely important trade routes and communications. Some Maya area cities came under the control of these foreign peoples during Terminal Classic times (A.D. 800-900), with resulting economic and political disruption and social unrest.

People such as a Pipil-speaking group from Mexico interrupted the calm of the Maya world by introducing militant attitudes, secular ideas, a pantheon of new deities, and an art style showing some influence of El Tajín and Teotihuacán. Also, new pottery was making its appearance from outside the Maya boundaries. Ceramic wares at Seibal and Altar de Sacrificios were imports from the Tabasco lowlands, replacing the Maya traditional pottery. New, non-Maya iconographic details became evident on Late Classic sculpture.

Possibly more important, in Terminal Classic times there was a shift in trade routes from the overland trails and riverine areas in the Lowland Maya region to the sea trade. This trade was made possible by improvements in canoe construction leading to the manufacture of much larger, seagoing crafts with sails and crews of oarsmen. It was then possible to ship at one time large quantities of such trade items as food produce, wood, minerals, and salt.

According to A. P. Andrews, the consumption of salt for a city such as Tikal, with its population of approximately fifty thousand, would require a minimum of forty tons of salt a year. Laboring people, however, needed several times this minimum. Obviously those persons who cornered the market for the transportation of salt and those cities, both coastal and inland, which established salt depots for marketing were in very favorable positions.

A major shift to coastal sea trade meant control of the market by new management. The Putun Maya, in the Tabasco area of the Gulf coast, were in the right geographical area to do this. The sea lanes extended from the Gulf coast around the Yucatán peninsula, into the Caribbean, and as far south as the region of the Motagua and Ulúa rivers. The Putun Maya management of the sea lanes and ports of call not only altered the economic and political control of the area but also introduced new ideas in religion,

13

social interaction, and a cultural awareness that displayed many foreign influences. Such a major shift of control must have been devastating to the older, theocratic ruling families who were well established in the major Maya cities.

Soon after the older Maya cities ceased to be effective focal points of Maya society, they were abandoned. Many Maya must have dispersed into regions ecologically more favorable for their survival, where they farmed, fished, and hunted until the Spanish conquest. Their dispersal could have taken them into the Guatemala Highlands along river, lake, and coastal areas or deeper into the Petén jungle. New Maya cities in other locations arose in Postclassic times. Once the old Maya cities were abandoned, the jungle quickly recaptured its hold on the territory, burying it in a network of lush tropical growth for another thousand years, until archaeologists and adventurers discovered the ruins.

The Maya territory is divided into four major areas: the Pacific Slope; the Highlands, north of the Guatemala and El Salvador Pacific Slope area; the Southern Lowlands, stretching along the Usumacinta River basin through the Petén to Honduras; and the Northern Lowlands, including the entire Yucatán Peninsula. Maya rulers of city-states—or, as recent research indicates, some rulers whose political control encompassed much more than city-states—were autonomous, but they did enjoy intercommunication and cooperation throughout the vast territory. With political alliances between such city-states as Tikal and Naranjo, Copán and Quiriguá, and Yaxchilán and Piedras Negras, a cultural, economic, and political homogeneity developed in the Maya world. Emblem glyphs, first identified by Heinrich Berlin, were acquired by the major cities, giving them political importance, even the status of a regional capital. Tikal and Yaxchilán were two of the earliest cities in the Southern Lowlands to acquire the status of capitals. Archaeological excavations at most of the major ceremonial centers indicate that a wealth of knowledge was spread from one Maya region to another on such subjects as writing, religion, the arts, and science.

Because of the long historical progression of expanding activities in the elaborate ceremonial cities, the increased demand for

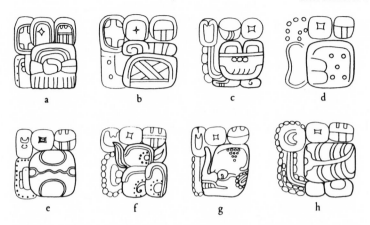

Emblem glyphs found on monuments identifying Maya cities. a: Tikal;
b: Naranjo; c: Yaxchilán; d: Piedras Negras; e: Palenque; f: Seibal;
g: Copán; h: Quiriguá. From Coe, *The Maya.*

exotic produce from distant territories and the consequent need for
communication and cooperation among the various city-states and
transportation and trade routes became important and integral
factors in Maya cultural development. The lords, priests, and scientists had constant need to communicate with each other. Architects and sculptors certainly engaged in lively exchanges of ideas
and were instrumental in fostering competitive activities in the
ceremonial centers. The position of the merchants was also important enough that they may well have been members of ruling
families. Rivers and the sea became the great highways for the
Maya. Rafts and canoes, some with sails, were used for transportation on these waters. Paved *sacbeob* (causeways) also served as
important communication links from one area to another nearby,
such as those between Kabáh and Uxmal and between Cobá and
Yaxuná. Footpaths through the jungle were also used, and on some
of these one might see a group of servants and advisers accompanying a lord, priest, or merchant in a wooden litter. Narrative

15

scenes on pottery and wall murals depict such journeys through the jungles.

Except for metals, natural resources were abundant in the Maya territory. Much of Petén and the Yucatán Peninsula rests on a bed of limestone which yields no metals. Limestone was extremely important, however, as a building material for the cities and towns. It was also an important stone for carved monuments. Sandstone and andesite were sometimes used where limestone was not available. Flint, jade, and obsidian were fashioned into important trade items. Jade was especially valuable and was considered much more precious than any other single item that one could own.

The basis of the economy was agriculture. In the Guatemala Highlands the soil was especially fertile. Corn was the main crop, but other produce was grown, especially beans, squash, peppers, and tomatoes. Cacao, a luxury for the rich, was grown along the Pacific Slope and in Belize, Chiapas, and Tabasco. Various fruits, such as the breadnut, plum, papaya, guava, and coconut, could readily be harvested. The forest was a valuable source of raw materials for home and building projects, rubber for the ball game, resin for religious ceremonies, and barks and leaves for paper and dyes. From the coastal areas of northern Yucatán, as well as the Pacific coast, the most important trade commodity was salt, also found in the Northern Highlands. Shells, fish, and other marine life were significant trade goods for both food and ceremonial use.

In the Maya territory slash-and-burn agriculture was practiced, and this system is still being used today. Once the land was cleared by burning, crops could be planted. In the Northern Lowlands the porous limestone base, in which water cannot be retained, causes the land to be so dry that only scrub vegetation is present. Except where a system of irrigation was practiced, using water from cisterns and cenotes, the yield in agricultural produce was very sparse in those areas.

Although the Maya civilization had its beginnings around 2500 B.C., it was not until much later, approximately 600 B.C., that we can see in various sectors of the Maya area a continuous evolution of ceremonial centers, with their templelike structures and palaces surrounded by other buildings. By Late Preclassic times (300 B.C.–A.D. 250) craftsmen in such ceremonial centers as Uaxactún and Tikal in the Petén were using stone for building and for the carving of fine monuments. Stucco decoration was in vogue at Tikal as well as at El Mirador during this time, and visitors today can see large stucco mask forms on buildings in the North Acropolis at Tikal. At this early time ceremonial centers were already the nucleus of the Maya community. Plazas were designed to enhance the temples. Palace buildings and homes for important personages were built around series of courtyards close to the ceremonial centers. Early temple buildings were laid on rectangular stone platforms or low, stepped pyramids. The actual temples in Preclassic times were constructed for the most part of perishable materials, but postholes on the tops of these platforms indicate their size and the manner of construction. This early kind of community planning set the pattern for the great ceremonial centers built during the Classic Period (A.D. 300–900).

Maya dwellings of today show little change from those built two thousand years ago. From the beginning houses were extremely functional. The high roof, made of thatch, and the thick adobe sidewalls ensured a cool dwelling place in an environment that was extremely hot and humid.

The corbeled vault, developed as early as Late Preclassic times, became an integral part of Maya architecture during Classic times, and was a possible outgrowth of the high-peaked thatched roofs used by these people for their homes from earliest times. Vaulted entrances to plazas and patios, vaulted arches leading to cities, and vaulted rooms and porticoed chambers are prominent features of Maya architecture. Excavations to date have not revealed the use of a true keystone. Methods of vaulting were highly varied to accommodate the shape of the arch or door. Also, there were many regional differences in the way stones were cut for vaulting. At Palenque the use of the trilobate arch in the East Court of the Palace is a fine example of Maya engineering expertise. At Uxmal the stonecutters employed interlocking shaped stones to strengthen the arch. Craftsmen of the Northern Lowlands also commonly used a boot-shaped stone to strengthen a larger doorway. These struc-

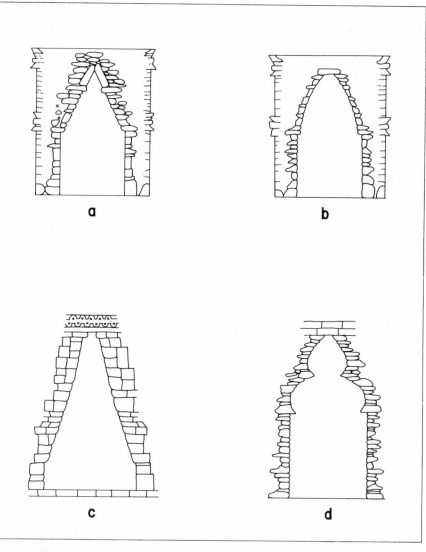

Corbeled arches. The Maya were ingenious in the many different ways in which they constructed the corbeled arch, or vault. These four doorways are only a sampling. a: Nunnery, Chichén Itzá; b: Uaxactun, showing curved soffit slopes; c: entrance to Palace of the Governor, Uxmal; d: trilobate arch, Palenque Palace. After Morley, The Ancient Maya.

tural stones were then covered with a thin veneer of mosaic stones that became a part of the exterior decoration of the building cornice.

A system of recording in hieroglyphics had its beginnings outside the Maya area as early as Middle Preclassic times (800–300 B.C.). Early glyphs can be seen on monuments at Olmec sites in Tabasco and Veracruz. In Monte Albán the recording of dates and inscribing of glyphs, as yet undeciphered, were performed at a very early time. The Maya used some of these rudimentary glyphs but developed many other glyphic forms until their system of writing became the most advanced in the Americas. For the most part their glyphic symbols combine logograms with affixes that represent phonetic complements. Some glyphs can be read phonetically. As it developed, Maya writing displayed increasing phoneticism.

A glyph consists of several component parts: a main glyph form with associated smaller forms that may be affixes representing adjectives, adverbs, or other modifying factors. Sometimes two glyphs are combined to form a single block and thus alter the meaning of the individual glyphs. Many variant forms were used for the main symbol of a glyph, thereby complicating the deciphering. For instance, a numeral may be represented by dots and bars, by a head variant, or by a full-figure variant. Scholars doing research on Maya glyphs are slowly unraveling this cumbersome system of writing. Even though there is much more work to be done in deciphering the glyphs, significant information has been gained from them in regard to Maya knowledge of astronomy and calendrics and Maya gods and ceremonies, as well as historical data.

Monuments such as stelae and altars were being carved during Preclassic times and became extremely important during the Classic Period in ceremonial centers at such cities as Copán, Quiriguá, Tikal, and Piedras Negras. On these monuments are finely carved glyphs commemorating events. The Maya had an obsession with carving dedicatory monuments. Stelae were erected to commemorate the fifty-two-year cycle as well as intervals of twenty and ten years. As the decline of the Maya became imminent, monuments were erected at five-year intervals at some centers. In many areas each stela was usually accompanied by a round, square, or oblong "altar," some carved with figures and hieroglyphs and others left

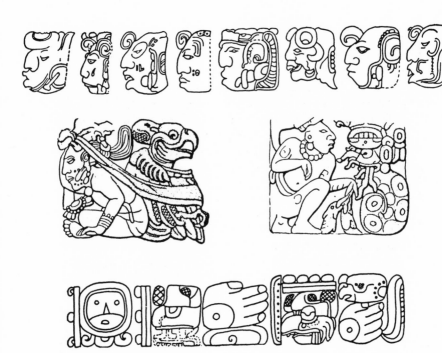

Maya glyphs. Top: The Maya artists had many ways of expressing the same number. These head variant glyphs represent the number 8; a bar and three dots express the same number, and a full-figure glyph can also mean 8. The great number of variations for numbers and words adds to the difficulty of deciphering the Maya script. Center, left: A full-figure glyph for the Baktun time period. The head variant is a bird. Stela D, Copán. Center, right: A full-figure glyph for the Tun time period. The head variant is attached to a serpent's body. Hieroglyphic Stairway, Copán. Bottom: Glyphs may also be grouped as phrases; this one is from Tikal. From J. Eric S. Thompson, Maya Hieroglyphic Writing: An Introduction.

plain. Some were shaped like mythological creatures; others resembled real animals. Their exact purpose is still unknown.

In some areas the Maya carved very large panels of glyphs for their buildings, and the largest of these can be seen on the rear wall of the Temple of the Inscriptions at Palenque. The longest of all known hieroglyphic inscriptions is carved on the facing of the beautiful Hieroglyphic Stairway at Copán. Both of these inscriptions contain historical data: royal family lineages, the dates for the ascent of the various Maya rulers, their deaths, and the marriage alliances of their children, as well as other events of the time. There are glyphs on stairways throughout the Maya territory. The Maya also recorded much of their history, scientific discoveries, and religious data in books. Unfortunately, the damp tropical forests were devastating to the fragile paper; moreover, the Spanish conquerors destroyed all of the Maya literature they could find. Only four Maya books (codices) survive today: the *Codex Dresden,* the *Codex Paris,* the *Codex Tro-Cortesianus* (also called *Codex Madrid*), and the *Codex Grolier.* The first three have been in European collections since the Spanish conquest.

Eight hundred years of Preclassic cultural development set the stage for the Maya Classic florescence. Sometime between A.D. 250 and 300 a new surge of activity permeated the great ceremonial centers. Architects were finding new ways to build greater palaces and temples, structures much more complex than those built in Preclassic times. Architectural detail showed new refinements in the relationship of one tectonic member to another; in the clean, crisp method of cutting stone; and in the exquisite expressions of the human figures in stucco relief on piers, walls, and roof combs of buildings. Roof combs, used in many sites throughout the Mayan area, gave height and emphasis to building façades. New techniques in the stone mosaic decorating the façades of temples and palaces were also introduced during the Late Classic Period. Buildings were plastered and painted at various times throughout Maya history. Wall paintings, in brilliant colors, decorated both the exterior and the interior of many of the Maya structures.

Much has been written on the dark, dismal, small rooms in temples and palaces that are said to be damp and unsuitable for human habitation. These opinions are based on modern Western standards and on observations at ceremonial centers as they are today. In the thousand years since their abandonment, mosses, lichens, and algae have encrusted buildings and monuments at the ceremonial centers, and the encroaching tropical forests have enveloped them, causing dampness and disintegration. During Classic times the forests were kept cut back, and the plazas, courtyards, and buildings were completely plastered with fine lime and painted. With the abundance of labor, especially slave labor from wartime raids, this kind of maintenance was possible and was continuous at the ceremonial centers. As an example, the interior of Temple 22 at Copan was covered with twenty-five successive coats of plaster. Walls were also painted in brilliant hues of green, yellow, orange, red, and blue that made them glisten in the sunlight. Thus preserved, the interiors of rooms were dry, bright, and cheerful.

The modern custom of using many different kinds of rooms for habitation was unknown to the Maya. Their glory and prestige lay not in the number and furnishings of rooms but in the public ceremonies and festivals. Temple and palace rooms must have had multiple uses. Sitting, eating, and sleeping could easily be arranged in a single room, much as they are in Maya houses today, and archaeological evidence in scenes on wall murals and pottery indicates very sparse furnishings. The many benches in the temples and palaces suggest that these were used for sitting and sleeping, while the recessed areas served as storage places for blankets, cushions, and portable tables. Traditionally the Maya kept cooking facilities separate from living quarters. In some palaces such conveniences as latrines, running water, steam baths, and fireplaces were provided.

With the emergence of the Classic Period ceramic pottery took on new shapes, and there was extensive production of ceramic ware throughout the Maya area. Vases were painted with polychrome decorations: narrative scenes depicting the lords of the Maya realm, a pantheon of Maya deities, animals, and glyphic inscriptions. A number of the most superb painted vases, with handsomely executed brushstrokes, were made at Ratinlixul and Chama, little-known sites north of the Guatemala Highlands.

Although we associate fine jade carving with Olmec times, some of the most magnificent jade pieces were carved during the Late Classic Period (A.D. 600-900). The largest Maya jade carving found to date came from a recent excavation at Altun Ha, in Belize. This amazingly large carved head, depicting the Maya sun god, Kinich Ahau (God G), weighs nine pounds seven ounces.

Carved figures and animal forms are rare in Maya jade. An unusual carving, discovered during excavations at Tikal, is that of a crouching jaguar weighing three and a half pounds. Most jade was carved into ornaments for the ruling families and priests. Important merchants also wore jade. Some of the carving is extremely delicate and certainly tested the skill of the lapidary: all his tools for shaping, grinding, and polishing were made of stone, wood, or bone. Some of the finest jade carvings, and the most numerous, have been found in the Guatemala Highlands at Kaminaljuyú and Nebaj. Many Maya jade pieces have also been found in the cenote at Chichén Itzá. Two of the most important burials in the Americas, in which great quantities of carved jade were discovered are at Tikal (Burial 116) and in the Temple of the Inscriptions at Palenque, the famous tomb discovered by Alberto Ruz Lhuillier. Probably jade, obsidian, and other trade goods could have been given as tribute to ruling families in the major cities.

Many new discoveries in the sciences, such as methods of computing the moons and the tropical year, originated in the greater Maya cities, and the information was quickly passed on to other Maya centers. The spirit of cooperation in endeavors of science, religion, construction, and festival ceremonies is evident throughout the Maya area. Also, hieroglyphic texts, stylistic influences, and religious homogeneity indicate some degree of peace and tranquillity among the various city-states. On the other hand, one can assume that border skirmishes, raids, wars, and human sacrifices were all very important to the Maya at certain times. The Bonampak murals well illustrate the kind of raid one village may have made on another and its effect. Also, there is evidence of human sacrifice at some burial sites where important dynastic rulers were entombed, both at Palenque and at Tikal.

Ceremonial centers were constantly being enlarged to commemorate various events or time cycles. A new building program was often inaugurated at the death of a great ruler, the ascendancy of a new lord, the discovery of a new computation in astronomy, or the birth of a new deity. New ceremonial centers were sometimes constructed, but the architects were more likely to build a much larger building over an existing structure. When this was done, the area around the walls of the smaller building was filled in with rubble, and often the original structure was left intact, much to the advantage of future archaeologists. Superimposition of this type continued throughout Maya history, and it is not unusual to find many superimpositions on a single structure. For instance, the House of the Magician at Uxmal has five superimpositions, and the North Acropolis at Tikal has nineteen earlier versions beneath it. Mesoamerica is unique in the world of archaeology in this particular type of architectural construction.

Considering the amount of activity carried on at a large ceremonial center, there must have been many schools and training centers for youth. The sons of the elite had to be able to read and write, learn the achievements in science and the arts, study architecture, master mathematics, memorize the rituals of religious practice, and understand the laws and mores of their society. Schools for the elite were probably restricted to sons of noble and merchant families. Training schools were needed for apprentices in other occupations such as those of scribes, accountants, merchants, masons, weavers, lapidaries, sculptors, painters, actors, dancers, and musicians. Many of these occupations formed a basis for additional social groupings and created a bridge between the elite and the laboring class. Thus the Maya social structure was not a two-class society but had varying levels of social groupings according to skills and knowledge needed for occupational specialization. Many of the occupations were inherited, not unlike the way craft guilds operated in medieval Europe. Mobility in Maya society from one status to another would not seem to have been an easy matter.

Little is known of Maya religion during Classic times. The codices, monuments, temples, and pottery give us some idea, however, of the pantheon of gods and their importance. Scholars have relied on such sources as Bishop Diego de Landa's *Relación de las cosas de Yucatán,* the *Popul Vuh,* and *Annals of the Cakchiquels* for information on Maya religion during the Late Postclassic Period. Generally speaking, most Maya gods were associated with forces of nature and had dual identities. They represented good or evil, male or female, animal or human, or a combination of both forms, and presided over night or day. This multiplicity, together with the changes in the gods over the long history of the Maya, makes it difficult to reconstruct the general pattern of their religion. Many of the gods were linked to the cardinal points and were associated with various colors.

Some of the gods served several purposes and had changing functions and forms. Chac, the rain god, for example, was also a reigning deity of winds and sometimes was depicted with symbols of death. The young maize god Yum Kaax who became so important at Copán, was also the embodiment of the ideal in male beauty; he served an additional function as protector of newly married couples. Ah Puch, the god of death and lord of the underworld, was also the malevolent god of the Maya. He opposed fertility and was often accompanied by animals of ill omen: the Moan bird (screech owl), and dog. Another important deity was Itzamná, the sky god, who had many attributes but was usually depicted as a toothless old man with sunken cheeks and a hooked nose. His wife, Ix Chel, was the moon goddess and protector of women in childbirth. At the time Cortés landed on the island of Cozumel, the shrine for this goddess was one of the most popular along the Quintana Roo coast. Other important gods were Kinich Ahau, the sun god; Xanam Ik, god of the North Star; and Ek Chuah, the war god.

The complicated Maya pantheon of gods becomes more so when they are related to the Maya cosmos. The thirteen heavens, ruled by sky deities, and the nine underworlds, ruled by the lords of the night, were also ritualistically significant in Maya calendrics. Afterlife was an important concept of the Maya religion, and apparently most persons expected to go to paradise. Formal rites accompanied by fasting and feasts certainly were an integral part of life at the ceremonial centers. Religious rituals, cycles, and ceremonies perpetuated by lords and priests became a great fascination, inspiration—and ensnaring bondage—for the masses of people who labored to build the tallest of all pyramid temples in the world.

The Maya ceremonial centers showed marked changes during the Postclassic Period (A.D. 900–1500). Because of political unrest, movements of large numbers of Mexicanized peoples into the Maya area, and the emergence of new city-states with a new ruling class, ceremonial centers became more secular, fortified, and militant. These changes can be seen in such Maya cities as Tulum, on the east coast of Quintana Roo; at Mayapán, in Yucatán; and in the Guatemala Highlands at Iximché and Mixco Viejo. In the six hundred years of Postclassic development there was not one Maya ceremonial center that achieved the grandeur, the excellence of workmanship, or the accomplishments in the sciences or arts of the Classic Period centers.

With the entrance of the Spanish conquistadors the Maya people witnessed the complete destruction of their literature, religion, and great works of art and experienced tragic decimation by warfare and disease.

2 The Pacific Slope: Monte Alto, El Baúl, and Las Ilusiones

Pantaleón, El Bilbao, Los Tarros, Monte Alto, Las Ilusiones, Abaj Takalik—these names have taken on new meaning to the townspeople along the Pacific coastal plain. These large property holdings, called fincas, are yielding some of the more recent archaeological finds from the systematic excavations of scientists. Sugarcane fields and coffee plantations along the Pacific Slope in Guatemala, only hours south of Guatemala City, still hold great archaeological treasures far beneath the surface soil.

A great number of large, boulder-like sculptures have been uncovered at Finca Monte Alto and other neighboring fincas. One of the large heads was found at the Finca El Transito by two children. Like many other such sculptures, this one has closed eyes, full lips, long ears, and a round face. In these heads the sculptor expresses an energetic inner force enhanced by the simplicity of the sculptural line. Many of these sculptures represent the heads or full figures of plump, chubby persons. They have been found in association with ancient mounds that must be the remains of very old religious ceremonial centers. Future excavations here may give us a clearer idea of the size and configuration of these early ceremonial centers and how they functioned.

Many of the large monolithic stones from the Finca Monte Alto have been moved to the village square in the little town of La Democracía, a most arbitrary and unbecoming location. A little museum in this village houses other, small early stone carvings.

For many decades the large carved boulders have been appearing along the Pacific Slope as far south as El Salvador. The Kaminaljuyú site in Guatemala City has also yielded many sculptures carved in the same style. A typical sculptured full figure is characterized by a barrel-shaped body; a baby face, usually with closed eyes; arms and legs simplified to ribbonlike bands wrapped

Large heads without bodies are the most common form of boulder sculpture along the Pacific Slope. Their purpose and exact dating are unknown. Some may be portrayals of rulers. Such boulder sculptures as these are reminiscent of the monumental stone sculptures carved by the Olmecs during Middle Preclassic times. The head is usually bald and has puffy lips and closed eyes. The stone is dark-gray basalt. Late Preclassic.

around the obese body; undifferentiated gender; and nudity or scant clothing. The carving is executed with a minimum of sculptural planes, and the back of the boulder is usually not carved. On some stones the ears, nose, and eyes are little more than line etchings, while other features of the sculptures are in high relief. A dark-gray volcanic stone, basalt, found in natural boulder form on the terrain, was utilized for these carvings.

Olmec sites in Veracruz and Tabasco have been credited with the earliest monumental sculpture in Mesoamerica. The major

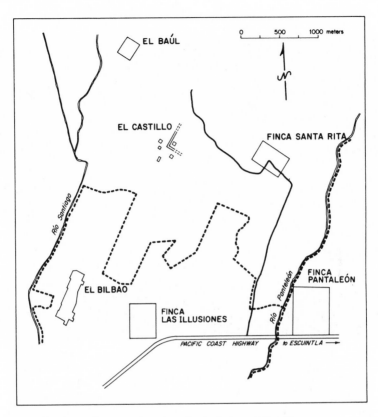

Pacific Coast fincas and archaeological sites. After Parsons.

centers are at La Venta, Tres Zapotes, and San Lorenzo. Their sculpture is characterized by monumental size, sophisticated carving techniques, and simplicity of form. Many of the heads and altars of the Olmec are much larger than any of those on the Pacific Slope in Guatemala. The ceremonial centers in the Olmec heartland were constructed in the Middle Preclassic Period.

The Olmec colonized or controlled areas very far from their major Gulf coast cities. They had a tremendous trade network that extended from the Gulf coast to the Valley of Mexico and then south into the rich mineral area of the Río Balsa. Another

29

Large boulder-type sculptures are found over a large part of the Pacific Slope and in the Guatemala Highlands. Many of the stones have been moved into the park at the village of La Democracia from the surrounding fincas where they were discovered. In this sculpture the subject is obviously lying on his back, and the legs and arms are sculptured in "wraparound" planes with little detail. This sculpture, Monument 2, was found at Monte Alto. Late Preclassic.

trade route crossed the Tehuantepec isthmus, turned south along the Pacific coastal plain and piedmont, and continued farther south to the region of El Salvador and Nicaragua. They wanted not only to control the sources of raw minerals but also to manage transportation and establish markets along these trade routes. Archaeological evidence reveals many forms of material culture at such sites as Abaj Takalik and Las Victorias.

Many of the hallmarks of the Olmec of Late Preclassic times

A number of boulder sculptures have been discovered on the finca Monte Alto. Adjacent fincas such as El Transito and Nuevo are also known for this type of sculpture. The face of this head (Monument 3 from Monte Alto) suggests a feline deity associated more often with Olmec sculpture than with Maya. Late Preclassic.

are noted at such sites as Cerro de las Mesas and Izapa; Abaj Takalik and Monte Alto, along the Pacific Slope of Guatemala; and Kaminaljuyú, in the Guatemalan Highlands. At this time a new artistic expression was evolving in sculptured monuments and in hieroglyphic writing.

The most important stylistic influence on the Pacific Slope in the Late Preclassic Period came from Izapa, a small ceremonial center in Mexico, just north of the Guatemala border. Izapa is the type site for the style of the same name, although it may have originated in the Veracruz area. During Late Preclassic and Proto-classic times (300 B.C.–A.D. 300) the Izapa style influenced cultures in the southern end of Mexico, the Pacific Slope of Guatemala, and the Highlands at Kaminaljuyú. Izapa-styled monuments have some Olmec traits, such as scrollwork skies or clouds, the flame-scroll brow, a motif resembling the Saint Andrew's cross, and scenes framed by a jaguar's jaw. Characteristics strictly Izapan also appear, however, such as deities descending from the sky, winged figures, U-shaped symbols, and the long-lipped god. The Izapa site was abandoned at the end of Late Preclassic times, but some elements of the style influenced Classic Maya sculpture.

Recent research by John A. Graham at Abaj Takalik, on the Pacific Slope south of Izapa, will no doubt throw new light on the cultural development of the Maya during the Preclassic and Proto-classic periods. Monuments found here fall into three categories. The first is the boulderlike monument, Olmec in style, possibly carved in Middle to Late Preclassic times. There is no concrete evidence revealing their exact date, however. The second category is that of the Izapa-styled monuments, and the third category includes the early Maya monuments. Stela 5, Stela 2, and an associated altar, all of which are in the Maya style, are monuments from the first century B.C. or earlier, according to Graham. Even though the early Maya monuments sometimes overlap in date with the Izapa site sculptures, the Izapa development seems to be separate. There are motifs and symbols on the monuments, however, some of them Olmec in origin, that were shared by the Maya and the Izapa people. The Izapa-styled sculptures are narrative, with human, animal, and zoomorphic content. Rarely are dates or glyphs found on these monuments. The Maya sculptures for the most part

Monument 28 at the finca Las Ilusiones is one of many sculptures adjacent to the finca headquarters. Not far from here is the Cotzumalhuapa site, which is believed to be Late Classic.

Monument 30 is in the town of El Baúl. This is one of a number of sculptures in the Cotzumalhuapa style of carving and glyphic writing. The style is associated with the Nahuatlized Pipil-speaking culture, active toward the end of the Late Classic Period.

Monument 13 at El Baúl appears to portray the head of a bearded man. Heads of this kind may have been tenoned into the façades of buildings as decoration. Lee Parsons has carried out fieldwork in this general area in the hope of establishing a chronology. Middle to Late Classic.

depict historical persons, and dates and other glyphs are usually included.

The next major influence on the Pacific Slope, in Guatemala and as far south as Honduras and El Salvador, was from the Mexican area. During the Middle and Late Classic periods (A.D. 400-900), invading or migratory peoples speaking Pipil (an archaic form of Nahuatl) from the Mexican central highlands and Veracruz occupied the area. The Pipil-speaking people were imbued with the Classic culture from El Tajín and Teotihuacán. In particular, the Fincas Las Ilusiones, El Bilbao, El Baúl, Pantaleón, Los Tarros, El Castillo, and Santa Rita were most affected by this last major stylistic influence. Lee Parsons, who has carried out archaeological research along the Guatemala slope, refers to this style as Cotzumalhuapa. The style is characterized by speech scrolls, non-Maya glyphs, ball-game players in association with death manikins, sun disks, sky deities, and human sacrifice. The area seems to have been in political turmoil for many centuries before the Late Classic Period. The economically important coastal cacao crops may have been a contingent factor during these turbulent times. It is also significant that the collapse of Teotihuacán coincided with the Pipil incursion.

A few miles north of Monte Alto is the site of El Baúl. Today there is little indication of the old ceremonial center. The earliest of the sculptures have been removed to the nearby village, where they can be seen in a little park. Sculptures include heads of men, mythological beings, deities, and various animal forms. These decorative elements may have enhanced panels in walls, cornices, moldings, doorjambs, or lintels. Large carved figures have shanks, suggesting that they were tenoned into the walls. These sculptures are carved in the Cotzumalhuapa style.

The earliest dated stela in the Maya area, Monument 1, with a dedication date of A.D. 36, is in El Baúl. The earliest non-Maya, dated stela [Stela C] found thus far is at Tres Zapotes, in Veracruz; it has a dedication date of 31 B.C. Monument 1 at El Baúl has some motifs carved in the Izapa style, but stylistically the monument is Maya and depicts a Maya ruler with accompanying Maya glyphs. There is much Preclassic pottery and sculpture on all the surrounding fincas. Predominant, however, is the Cotzumalhuapa sculpture of Middle and Late Classic periods.

Monument 3, in a sugarcane field not far from El Baúl, is an example of the monumental style of sculpture that may have been introduced by the Pipil-speaking migrants who moved into the Pacific Slope area during Middle and Late Classic times. The wrinkled brow is reminiscent of Plumbate effigy jars made near the border between Guatemala and Mexico in the Early Postclassic Period. Today local Indians worship here.

Most of the Cotzumalhuapa-styled sculptures are found at the fincas Las Ilusiones, Pantaleón, and El Bilbao. These plantations grow coffee as their chief crop, but in recent years sugarcane has also been grown. Even cacao, at one time economically important, is still grown here. The area is heavy in rainfall, creating a tropical growth, lush and exuberant. Sculptures at Pantaleón are in the Cotzumalhuapa style and can be seen today at the finca headquarters. Many of the sculptures and other artifacts at El Bilbao have been removed from the major site area, Monument Court, to the headquarters of the finca, which is owned by José Ricardo Muñoz Gálvez. In its early history this finca was known as Bilbao, a name used for the title of the two-volume manuscript by Lee Parsons on the archaeology of the Pacific Slope. Bilbao is also the name used for the type site encompassing the entire area.

On Finca El Baúl, locally referred to as Finca San Francisco, there are still two very large monumental sculptures in the Cotzumalhuapa style hidden away in a clump of trees surrounded by a sugarcane plantation. One of these heads, Monument 3, is that of a wrinkled old man. Today the Maya populace uses this monument as a shrine. It is not unusual to see a soothsayer there saying prayers while he swings an incensory smoking with copal. Offerings of flowers and sometimes chicken eggs, which are broken over the stone, are left.

In the year 1880 a very important group of more than thirty Late Classic stone monuments, all carved in the Cotzumalhuapa style, were removed from Finca El Bilbao. Eight of the monuments are the famous Cotzumalhuapa stelae, now housed in the Völkerkunde Museum, in Berlin. The eight large stelae are the finest carved monuments of their kind from the Pacific Slope. After five years of arduous labor spent in transporting these sculptures to the coast, they were shipped to Germany. Unfortunately, one of the stelae was lost in the ocean when it was being transferred from the shore to the ship. Guatemala lost many of its great art treasures when explorers and adventurers carted them off around the turn of the century. The illegal robbing of mounds for artifacts is still going on today in both Mexico and Central America.

The Cotzumalhuapa stelae show decided Mexican influence in the use of speech scrolls and other symbolic motifs not associated with the Maya. The carvings, in low relief, depict ritual scenes associated with ball-game ceremonies, and they bear similarities to carvings at El Tajín. The monuments were taken from the Sunken Court, where the ball court is located. The site has produced no superstructures for the court, so commonly used by the Maya throughout the Highlands and Lowlands. In the museum in Guatemala City replicas can now be seen of two of these Cotzumalhuapa monuments.

Mushroom-shaped stones, as well as metates, mortars, and other stone objects, have frequently been dug up on the fincas when fields were being prepared for planting. The carving of mushroom stones, in various sizes and styles, started in Preclassic times, possibly as early as 500–300 B.C., and continued into the Postclassic Period (A.D. 900-1200). The earliest kind can be identified by a groove around the top. Carved during Preclassic times, this kind may also have a stem carved with an effigy figure, and the base of the mushroom may be a tripod or a square. During Classic times the mushroom had no groove, and the stem was plain. This was the general pattern, but it was marked by regional differences.

In Kaminaljuyú nine metates and manos were found with nine mushroom stones dating to the Miraflores stage (300 B.C.–A.D. 150). This number suggests a relationship of the mushroom stones and metates with the nine Lords of the Night, or Underworld, as depicted in Maya art and mythology.

Mushroom-shaped stones are found in the Maya area along the Pacific Slope, in the Guatemala highlands, and in the Eastern Lowlands as far south as El Salvador. From the Spanish chronicles we know that mushrooms were used for various kinds of ritual ceremonies among the Aztec, Mixtec, Tarascan, and other groups in the Mexican highlands. The hallucinogenic mushrooms were ground on a metate, water was added, and the mixture was drunk for specific cult rituals. Stone mushrooms have not been found where similar present-day cults exist. It is not even certain that these stones represented mushrooms; they may have represented the phallus or had some other meaning.

No significant superstructures of ancient ceremonial centers are visible in the area of the Pacific Slope today. The largest number of mounds, seventeen in all, are on the Finca El Bilbao. Little is known regarding these mounds and the significance in ancient times of the structures they cover.

Continued archaeological excavations and research along the Pacific Slope should unfold more of the developmental stage of the three major art styles and the ceremonial centers with which they were associated.

3   The Petén: Tikal

Mahogany, cedar, and chicle trees rise two hundred feet high to screen the Petén jungle, as seen from the air, but the five great roof combs on the pyramids at Tikal pierce the crest of the tropical forest. The landing field for planes is adjacent to the Tikal Museum and within walking distance of the Tikal ceremonial center. With the excellent manual *Tikal: A Handbook of the Ancient Maya Ruins*, by William R. Coe, it is possible to see Tikal on your own, provided you have a few days to relax and explore the many trails that meander through some of the more remote regions of the forest. Both howler and spider monkeys sweep through the jungle in mid-afternoon just behind the Central Acropolis. Their noise can be heard for miles. Keelbilled toucans, motmots, and parrots are some of the many birds that give color to the jungle environment. The early afternoon, when the air is clear, the trails are in shadow, and the temperature is comfortable, is the best time to explore the remains of this once thriving ceremonial city that was occupied for over a thousand years.

Tikal was a functioning city as early as Preclassic times (600 B.C.–A.D. 250). Ecologists believe that the Petén jungle may have been savannah country even as late as Classic times. The area became the dense jungle forest it is today after the city was abandoned. This environmental change may have been due in part to climatic shifts. At its height, during the Late Classic Period (A.D. 600-900), Tikal had a dispersed population of no more than fifty thousand people, covering approximately 500 square miles. Tikal and Teotihuacán were the two largest urban centers in Mesoamerica during Classic times. Today the area of Tikal is a national park for the preservation of the archaeological zone, covering 222 square miles.

The Tikal site has been known since the seventeenth century.

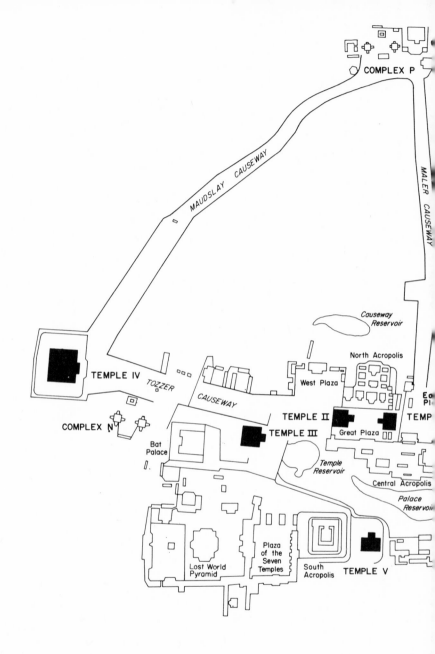

Tikal

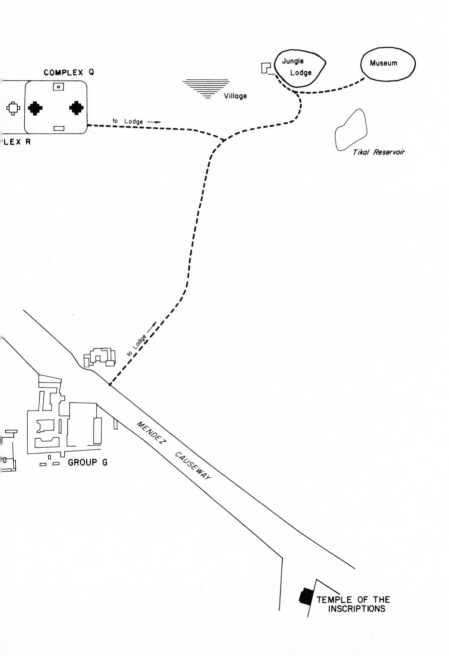

COMPLEX Q

LEX R

to Lodge →

≈≈≈≈ Village

Jungle Lodge

Museum

Tikal Reservoir

to Lodge

GROUP G

MENDEZ CAUSEWAY

TEMPLE OF THE
INSCRIPTIONS

In 1881–82, Alfred Maudslay executed detailed drawings that alerted adventurers and scholars to the possible wealth of the ruins. Teobert Maler explored and photographed the area in 1895 and again in 1904. Earlier, Gustav Bernoulli visited the area and had the lintels removed from Temples I and IV; these are now in the Museum für Völkerkunde, in Basel, Switzerland. Sylvanus G. Morley made many trips into the Petén between 1914 and 1928, and his scholarly contributions on Maya inscriptions are a monumental achievement.

It was in 1956 that the University of Pennsylvania inaugurated a bold and dramatic program for Tikal, directed first by Edwin Shook and later by William R. Coe, in which some of the major buildings were to be excavated and partly reconstructed. Fifteen years later, in 1971, their great work was concluded. Since then archaeological excavations have continued under the auspices of the Instituto de Antropología e Historia of Guatemala. Even though only a fraction of the area has been restored, the work involved was not unlike rebuilding a Maya city. The great care needed to excavate such an important zone as this can be appreciated only by watching the archaeologists at work, sifting every teaspoon of dirt over acres of land as they slowly piece together the remains of Maya history. The ruins of Tikal as we see them today are a testimonial not only to the Maya who built them but also to the many scholars who have worked here to restore a small part of the splendor that was once the great city.

The five great pyramids of Tikal give this ceremonial center a majestic grandeur unique among Maya cities. The height of the temples, crowned with tremendous roof combs; the complicated assemblage of the palace structures of the Central Acropolis; and the complexity of the chronology of the North Acropolis are staggering to anyone first visiting Tikal. In ancient times Tikal functioned mainly as a ceremonial center in which the aristocratic elite and their priests ruled, dictated, and directed the activities of the architects, builders, craftsmen, and laborers. All endeavors in the region of Tikal were directed to enhance the city, to glorify the gods, to amass wealth, and to acquire tribute for the ruling upper strata of society. To sustain this activity for over a thousand years demanded a well-disciplined peasantry.

Temple I is one of five major temple pyramids at Tikal. Temple IV, the tallest, towers 229 feet above ground level. Temple I, also known as the Temple of the Giant Jaguar, faces the Great Plaza. It was con-structed about A.D. *700.*

The best view of the North Acropolis at Tikal is that from the top of Temple I. Construction of the North Acropolis started in Preclassic times and continued through the Late Classic Period. The structures seen here today date from the Early Classic Period.

One of the two highest pyramids in the New World is Temple IV, whose roof comb is 229 feet high. As one approaches the Great Plaza, the impression is one of monumental scale. Temples I and II face each other from the ends of the plaza. The palace buildings are on the south, and the extraordinary North Acropolis looms over the whole expanse of the ceremonial center.

During the Late Preclassic Period and into the Protoclassic Period, El Mirador, a large city forty miles north of Tikal, was politically and economically the most powerful city in the Petén. The tallest pyramid in El Mirador is in the Danta Complex and rises to a height of 230 feet, approximately the same height as Pyramid IV in Tikal. Recent excavations at El Mirador reveal a splendid city in which the structures are decorated with large stucco masks. El Mirador first came under construction during the Middle Pre-classic Period and reached a peak in the Late Preclassic. It was abandoned at the end of the Protoclassic Period, approximately A.D. 300, at which time Tikal rose to power and dominated the Southern Lowlands from the beginning of the Early Classic Period. With the eruption of the Ilopango volcano in A.D. 200-250, much of the agricultural and mineral resources in what is now El Salvador, Honduras, and part of Guatemala was engulfed in tons of volcanic ash, causing a shift in population and disruption of the major trade routes. The eruption may have been an important factor in the cultural decline of the Maya in the Protoclassic Period.

Excavations in the North Acropolis of Tikal have proved exceedingly fruitful in revealing its early history. The area has eighty funerary temples and served as a necropolis from the Late Preclassic through the Early Classic periods. The earliest structures, making the beginning of the ceremonial center and excavated at the lowest level of the North Acropolis, are Preclassic buildings dating from 200 B.C. The Lost World Pyramid, west of Temple V, is also Preclassic. These dates indicate a long developmental period for the Maya at Tikal before the Early Classic Period commenced in A.D. 250. During this long period of time the acropolis went through innumerable changes. Early structures in this area were mostly temples. The style of architecture was already showing refinements, such as apron moldings, that would eventually evolve

Stucco sculptures decorate several Early Classic buildings in the North Acropolis at Tikal. This huge rain-god mask adorns part of the façade of Structure 5D-33 sub.

into the Classic style. Over the next six hundred years the North Acropolis was built over many times and was enlarged until it covered two and a half acres. Under this huge complex is buried a long history of past generations and their particular architectural accomplishments.

Structure 5-D-26 contained an Early Classic tomb (Burial 22) believed to be that of Tikal's ruler Jaguar Paw. His reign was followed by that of Curl Nose, who is portrayed on Stelae 4 and 18. It is quite possible that Burial 10 is that of Curl Nose. He died in A.D. 425 after ruling for forty-seven years. His son, Stormy Sky, was Tikal's greatest ruler in the Early Classic; his tomb is believed to be Burial 48. This tomb contained many objects that showed ties with Teotihuacán and Kaminaljuyú. On the tomb wall

49

was painted the date A.D. 456. Much of what is known about the dynastic succession has been the work of Coggins and Jones. The large pyramid (5D-33) built above this tomb was dismantled during the Tikal project as being unsafe. It was a Late Classic structure.

Throughout Mesoamerican history most of the buildings and monuments were painted in brilliant colors. Stucco decoration was used on some of the earliest buildings here. With the constant razing, enlarging, and adding of structures, the network of old buildings under the present plaza floor became a maze of architectural superimpositions.

At Tikal the Early and Late Classic periods are separated by a Middle Classic hiatus (A.D. 550-600) that was to affect the architecture as well as the social and economic aspects of the great city. The exact nature of the hiatus is unknown. The Teotihuacán civilization, especially that of the power-based city of Kaminaljuyú, with whom Tikal conducted important trade relations, came to an end at about this time. This major change could have disrupted trade routes, thus upsetting a balance in the political and economic systems at Tikal and other Maya cities. A similar crisis, mentioned above, occurred between the Late Preclassic and the Early Classic, when all trade routes were disrupted by the devastating eruption of the Ilopango volcano. Soon after the Early Classic crisis immense building programs were undertaken. It is possible that by this time the Maya had taken over many of the Teotihuacán trade routes after their withdrawal and reestablished their economic and political power over a much larger terrain.

This Late Classic Period (A.D. 600-900) witnessed a great population increase, and agricultural changes were necessary to accommodate food demands. It is now believed that in areas of large populations such as Tikal intensive agriculture was practiced in smaller plots, replacing to some degree the dominant swidden system used in Early Classic times. Terracing was practiced, and raised plots were used, both permitting double cropping. Irrigation canals are known in several locations. The breadnut tree, popularly called ramon *(Brosimum alicastrum)*, was also cultivated and became a staple food. Ramon nuts are highly nutritious and can be made into tortillas. The tree requires little care, lives for nearly a hundred years, and can support many more people than can corn.

The North Acropolis at Tikal provides a striking view of the Great Plaza, stretching into the distant jungle. Rising above the horizon is Temple V, the second-tallest pyramid at Tikal, towering 188 feet above ground level. Unrestored, the temple roof comb is covered with a lush green carpet of ferns, mosses, and tropical shrubs. The lofty roof combs at Tikal are the most massive of those in the Maya area. The Tikal architects did not pierce the roof comb, a common practice at other ceremonial centers such as Palenque, Uxmal, and Yaxchilán. The exterior of the roof comb is a solid mass, but the interior has a partly hollow core that is vaulted and sealed to lessen the weight of the comb on the temple walls. The tremendous weight of the comb made it necessary to build extremely heavy supporting walls, leaving little room for the actual temple. Stucco decorations in the form of heroic masks were added to the front panel of the roof comb, and this panel was then painted.

Although the Maya architects did not plan completely symmetrical ceremonial centers, at Tikal there is a particularly strong suggestion of a formal relationship of one building to another within the plazas, especially within the compounds of the twin pyramid complex.

The Great Plaza, which stretches over two acres, had four superimpositions of plaster over a period of six hundred years. Construction of the original plaza started as early as 150 B.C. William R. Coe, who directed most of the excavation and reconstruction of Tikal, estimates that the final resurfacing of the plaza was completed in approximately A.D. 700.

The north end of the plaza is dotted with stelae and altars. There are a great number of these monuments at Tikal, and some are beautifully carved, while others are uncarved or are in very poor condition. The Maya sculptures at Tikal are more conservative than the flamboyant baroque style so much in evidence at Copán. The earliest monument (Stela 29) excavated so far at Tikal has glyphs with the date A.D. 292. On the face of this monument is Tikal's emblem glyph (a symbol of a Maya city, possibly of a capital city).

At the base of the stairway to the Temple of the Inscriptions

The Great Plaza at Tikal. Temple I is on the left and the Central Acropolis is in the distance. Late Classic.

Although little remains of Stela 21 at Tikal, badly damaged during Late Classic times, the execution of the glyphs and of the man's foot attest to the sculptor's skill. The stela is near the Temple of the Inscriptions (Temple VI) and portrays Yax Kin (A.D. *736).*

(Temple VI) is Stela 21, one of the finest of the carved stelae at Tikal. The glyphs and the superb rendering of the foot of the standing ruler, Yax Kin (A.D. 736), illustrate the Classic Maya ideal of beauty in sculpture. This monument was found broken, with pieces scattered as far as half a mile away. The stela can now be admired in its partly restored condition. Other important stelae that reflect the artistry of the Tikal craftsmen are Stela 22, portraying a ruler of Tikal named Chitam, with a date of A.D. 771, in Complex Q; and Stela 16, portraying the great ruler Ah Cacau, dated A.D. 711, in Complex N. Ah Cacau is also portrayed on Stela 30 and on the lintel of Temple 1. His tomb (Burial 116) is famed for its rich treasure of jade, pottery, and many other artifacts, which can now be seen at the Tikal Museum.

Occasionally there is archaeological evidence of human sacrifice among the Maya. This is well illustrated in the temple murals at Bonampak, in the burial chamber under the Temple of the Inscriptions at Palenque, in a burial at Tikal, and elsewhere. Burial 10 in the North Acropolis at Tikal contained the remains of a ruler, possibly Curl Nose (Coggins), who died around A.D. 425. The remains of nine retainers who were killed for the occasion were found in the tomb. Another evidence of human sacrifice is found on an altar at the foot of Temple III. Carved on the side of the altar is a tripod bowl containing a human head. Near Temple IV at Complex N a circular monument, Altar 5, about five and a half feet in diameter, is carved with the figures of two rulers or priests standing behind an altar on which are placed a cranium and thigh bones. Other altars show carvings of bound prisoners (such as Altar 8 in Complex P) who could be persons who were sacrificed at the time the monument was dedicated.

In at least two instances howler and spider monkeys are represented on a stela (Stela 1 in the Tikal Museum) and on an altar (on the platform of the North Acropolis). Monkeys, common in this area, were subjects for artistic expression throughout Mesoamerica. During Late Classic times they were a favorite subject on Maya pottery. Monkeys were associated with promiscuity in Maya myths and are believed to have been used sometimes as a symbol of fertility, often having a strong phallic character.

Stela 16 at Tikal is of particular interest because of the intricate detail of the dress of this important ruler, Ah Cacan (A.D. 711). The tombstone-shaped stela is not unusual at Tikal and is associated with Late Classic sculpture. Nearby is Altar 5, associated with Stela 16.

Many of the ruined monuments at Tikal were deliberately broken or defaced by their own people. This seems to have been a common practice in several Maya ceremonial centers during Classic times. The destruction may have symbolized a form of sacrifice to the gods. Another possible reason for destroying or defacing monuments could be to "kill" the power of the ruler depicted on the monument. This practice may have been carried out at the time of the ascendancy of a new ruler. It is fortunate that this practice was not in vogue at Copán, the fairest of all Maya cities for heroic sculpture.

Temple I rises 170 feet from the East Plaza platform to the top of the roof comb. Since the area surrounding the structure is cleared all the way down to the original ground level, Temple I is the most impressive of the pyramids. It was built after the death of the ruler Ah Cacau. The single stairway, sweeping from the plaza to the building platform, without balustrades or ramps, is breathtaking. The view from the top of Temple I is unparalleled in the Petén. On the opposite side of the Great Plaza is Temple II, the wooden lintel of which seems to portray a standing woman with a long cape or dress. She may be the wife of Ah Cacau. In the distant jungle can be seen the roof combs of Temples III, IV, and V. Temple IV and the Danta Complex at El Mirador are the two tallest structures in the pre-Columbian world. Temple IV may have been constructed to honor Yax Kin Caan Chac, son of Ah Cacau. A date on the lintel is A.D. 741. His inauguration was earlier, in 734. Chitam, son of Yax Kin Caan Chac, is the last known ruler of this dynasty.

There is only a dirt trail to the top of Temple IV, the pyramid usually climbed by visitors. The roots of trees and small bushes give one a foothold while attempting this extremely steep climb. The pyramidal bases for these temples are quite similar; stepped terraces with apron moldings are the customary tectonic motif, but the number of terraces and the treatment of the corners vary. A single stairway was used to reach the summit of the pyramid. Each of the temples crowning the pyramids has one to three small, vaulted rooms. In most buildings one can see graffiti dating from Late Classic to Postclassic times. On the south side of Temple I

The Great Plaza at Tikal. The North Acropolis is on the right, and Temple II is at the end of the plaza. Temples III and IV can be seen on the horizon. Late Classic.

Temple II at Tikal, also known as the Temple of the Masks. At the top are three rooms similar in structure to those of Temple I. One of the original carved beams to the central lintel is preserved in the American Museum of Natural History, in New York. Late Classic.

is one of the smallest of all Maya ball courts, build during the Late Classic Period. Other ball courts are known at Tikal, the most unusual one being a triple court on the north side of the Plaza of the Seven Temples.

Dozens of burials of both ordinary and highborn persons have been excavated at Tikal. One of the most sumptuous graves (Burial 116), where lay the remains of the illustrious member of the opulent elite of Tikal, Lord Ah Cacan, was discovered at the base of Temple I. He died in Late Classic times and was buried with his ceremonial clothing, jewelry, and dozens of the most prized artifacts, including pottery vessels and bone objects carved with glyphs and ceremonial scenes. The graduated jade beads of his necklace, the jade bracelets, and other carved-jade adornments total 180

In Burial 195 at Tikal were found four identical stuccoed wooden figures of the Maya rain god. They are now in the Tikal Museum. The figures are sixteen inches high and date from about A.D. 600.

pieces that together weigh sixteen and a half pounds. Most of these great treasures are now on exhibit at the Tikal Museum. Also at the museum is a beautifully carved jade image of a lying or sleeping jaguar, weighing three and a half pounds. It was found in Burial 196, not far from Pyramid II, which may be the tomb of Ah Cacan's son Yax Kin. Another treasure in the museum is the set of four identical stuccoed wooden figures, each sixteen inches high, depicting the Maya rain god. The thin plaster is a pale blue. In working on these sculptures, the archaeologists left the restored areas white so that they could be easily distinguished from the original work. These sculptures were found with other artifacts in Burial 195 (A.D. 600).

Just beyond Temple II a dirt road leads to Temple III. Although a large portion of the temple on top of the pyramid has been restored, the pyramid rises into a luxuriant forest that completely encases it. The ascent to the top of the pyramid is no more difficult than the ascent to the top of Temple IV, the one usually climbed by visitors. The view is superb from the top, but the real reward of the climb is in seeing the carved lintel in the two-room temple. This wooden lintel and two beams of another in Temple I are the only remaining original carved lintels at Tikal. All the others were carted off many years ago to museums in Basel, London, and New York. Lintels were carved of sapodilla, a very hard, durable wood fairly resistant to insects. Although the lintel in Temple III is badly worm-eaten, the design can still be discerned. Covering an area of approximately fourteen square feet, the lintel is the largest of all at Tikal. Carved in bas-relief, the central personage stands in front of a throne with two accompanying figures on either side. Glyph panels flank the latter figures. The important person portrayed in the central panel, possibly Lord Chitam, is immense. He is dressed in jaguar skins, wears a headdress of a jaguar with quetzal feathers, and is adorned with jade pieces and shells. Because of the importance of the ceremonial dress on the central figure of the lintel, the temple is known as the Temple of the Jaguar Priest. Temple III rises to a height of 178 feet, considerably higher than Temple I or Temple II.

The Central Acropolis, adjacent to the south side of the Great

Temple III, at Tikal, looms 180 feet above the Petén forest floor; it is known also as the Temple of the Jaguar Priest. It has two rooms; between them is preserved the best carved lintel remaining at Tikal. It may portray the ruler Chitam. Construction here was started a little over one hundred years after Temples I and II were built.

The Central Acropolis at Tikal occupies four acres on the south side of the Great Plaza. Only part of this area, believed to have been the ruling families' or the priests' residence, has been excavated and restored.

This high corbeled vault is typical of many of the vaulted passages at Tikal, but the spindle-shaped vault beams are unusual. They are in the rear room of the Five-Story Palace in the Central Acropolis. Late Classic.

Plaza, contains more than four acres of palace structures centering around six courtyards. This acropolis offered ideal residences for the Tikal aristocracy. The many courtyards gave privacy for individual families, and all the buildings had a great number of rooms with vaulted chambers. Most of the Central Acropolis, occupied from Preclassic times, still lies buried fifty feet below ground level, for excavations here have not been extensive. Consequently, the visible buildings range from Early through Late Classic times. The few Early Classic buildings can be distinguished by the size of the cut stone: the stones used for Early Classic construction were somewhat smaller than those used for Late Classic structures. This change in the size of the cut stones can be seen on Structure 46, where the central building is of Early Classic date and the two side wings were added during Late Classic times.

In total, the Central Acropolis has forty-two buildings and hundreds of vaulted rooms. Most of the buildings face courtyards one story high, although a few buildings have more than one story. One of the more impressive buildings is the Maler Palace, seen at the south end of Court 2, the largest court on the west side of the Central Acropolis. This two-storied Late Classic structure was decorated with a frieze that encircled the building, but there is little indication of its remains today. Many of the buildings here have the original wooden lintels and crossbeams used in the vault. Rooms on the back of the Maler Palace face the huge reservoir that supplied the water for this part of the ceremonial center. As seen today, it is a deep ravine filled with jungle growth. Occasionally a beautiful fragile blue motmot will be seen flying over the lush tropical foliage.

The terrain on which the Central Acropolis was built is uneven. Consequently, the buildings and courtyards are on different levels, united by a maze of passages both inside and outside the palace structures. When the moon is full, this area becomes a splendid viewing platform from which to survey the Great Plaza. On such a night Tikal is transformed into a mystic city, glowing in the silvery-blue moonlight.

Adjoining the east end of the Central Acropolis are three buildings that show a decided influence from Teotihuacán, the great Classic civilization of Mexico. One of these buildings has been excavated and is partly restored. Mexican influence in architecture and trade items, such as pottery, is found in the Maya area at Tikal as well as at Kaminaljuyú, in the Guatemala Highlands. No doubt these two major cities of Early Classic times had an alliance for the procurement of natural resources, the management of trade routes, and the marketing of trade goods. It is conceivable that at Kaminaljuyú people from Teotihuacán controlled the distribution of such trade items as obsidian and jade found in the Guatemala Highlands. Kaminaljuyú could have held the workshops for these much-sought-after minerals and may have been the central dispersion city for all Teotihuacán trade goods. Well-established trade routes made possible a great interchange of luxury items from one cultural area to another. The transmittal of culture was a continuous process in Mesoamerica from earliest Olmec times through the Middle Preclassic Period (900–500 B.C.) and up to the Spanish conquest.

Four major causeways linked the various parts of the city of Tikal. Along the Maudslay Causeway is the limestone quarry used for the restoration of Tikal. An early-morning walk along the Méndez Causeway leads to the Temple of the Inscriptions (Temple VI), first discovered by Antonio Ortiz. The light at that hour makes the hieroglyphs on the roof comb and the cornice of the building more easily seen. The long inscription is believed to be a summary of the historical dynasties at Tikal. Mythological information is also present. In tracing the genealogy at Tikal, one finds that lineality was extremely important. Patrilineal descent seemed to be the rule, even though we know the particular importance of some of the women at Tikal. A hereditary ruling elite existed at least from the fourth century and may have extended even much further back in Tikal history. This kind of dynastic rule continued until the decline of the Maya civilization.

Besides the major causeways at Tikal, there are innumerable jungle trails uniting smaller plazas and complexes over the many acres in the major part of the ceremonial center. After a few days in Tikal there is time to see some of the more remote areas of the city as well.

There are seven twin-pyramid complexes at Tikal. The first

Complex Q at Tikal. Through the corbeled arch can be seen Stela 22 (A.D. 771), portraying Chitam, a ruler of Tikal. In front of the stela is Altar 10.

two date from the reign of Ah Cacau, the earlier being A.D. 613. This unique architectural development evolved in Tikal, and the only other Maya city with this kind of complex is Yaxhá, southeast of Tikal. The plan of the twin-pyramid complex is the same at all locations, but the size of the area and the constructions can vary. This complex is constructed on an elevated plaza covering an area of approximately five acres. Two pyramids are placed on the outer edge of the plaza, on an East-West axis. In front of the east pyramid is a group of plain stelae that may have been painted red at one time. On the south side of the plaza a nine-door structure faces into the court. The north side of the plaza has a walled enclosure with a vaulted arch for an entrance. In the center of the enclosure is a beautifully carved stela and altar. This enclosure may have had a thatched roof at one time. These unusual complexes must have served some new religious or ceremonial development

Stela 20 and Altar 8 were at one time associated with one of seven twin-pyramid complexes at Tikal. Although badly eroded, the standing figure, a portrayal of the ruler Yax Kin, can clearly be seen holding a war club. Behind him is a jaguar throne. The design on the altar is similar to others at Tikal

in which a bound prisoner lies on his stomach with his feet tied behind his back. The stela is dated A.D. *751. These two monuments have been removed to the National Museum of Archaeology and Ethnology, in Guatemala City.*

in Late Classic times. Best known of these is Complex Q, because of the extensive restoration here. Complex P is especially interesting because of the carving on Stela 20 and the companion Altar 8. The original monuments are now in the Archaeology Museum in Guatemala City; these two at Tikal are replicas.

The stelae in the twin-pyramid complexes have rulers sculptured on them, and sculptures in other locations at Tikal also depict rulers. Stela 22 portrays Lord Chitam (A.D. 771), Stela 16 portrays Ah Cacau (A.D. 711), Stela 31 portrays Stormy Sky (A.D. c. 426), and Stela 21, at the base of Temple VI, portrays Yax Kin (A.D. 734). Yax Kin is also portrayed on Stela 20 and on the wooden lintel from Temple IV. These are only a few of the portrayals of dynastic rulers at Tikal. Altars associated with stelae sometimes stand in front of them. Altar 8, in Complex P, and Altar 9, at the foot of the stairway to Temple VI, each have a carved figure of a bound prisoner with arms and legs tied behind his back. This is a frequent motif at Tikal and other Maya sites, indicative of wars and skirmishes among the Maya and possibly with non-Maya people as well. The taking of prisoners for use as slaves, and possibly for sacrifice, is known throughout Mesoamerican history.

It is quite possible that the ceremonial center at Tikal served as a capital for the people living in the surrounding countryside as far away as twenty to thirty miles from its center. The earliest appearance of Tikal's emblem glyph is on Stela 29 (A.D. 292). Smaller cities such as Naranjo and Aguateca were probably under the sovereignty of the Tikal ruling family, although the extent of political control from the capitals is unknown. It was at Tikal that the aristocrats directed the activities of their domain. The rank of the ruling family and possibly of priestly families was hereditary, and marriage alliances, promoting a social and political unity, were important among the elite of different cities. The stratified Maya society offered little class mobility. Paintings on pottery during Late Classic times suggest the relative status of various groups of people. The class of merchants, tradesmen, and craftsmen was more closely tied into the activities of the ceremonial center than were the peasants, whose farms were distant from the capital. After the farming season was over, the peasants were probably expected to join the slaves and other laborers in building and re-building the great ceremonial centers — a public-works program that continued for over a thousand years.

The Maya pattern of settlement in communities has been es-tablished by investigating the elevated platforms used as the foun-dations of all homes and other buildings at Tikal. Some of the houses were built of stone and mortar, but most were constructed of wooden frames of mahogany or cedar, walls of sticks covered with adobe, and roofs of palm thatch. The platforms for the houses were plastered. Maya houses of today are very similar to those built at this very early time.

There was no particular pattern to Maya burials. The graves of ordinary persons were simple, while the ruling class and upper middle class had more elaborate graves of stone.

Throughout the Maya area most burials of ordinary people were under the platforms of the houses, but sometimes the person was buried at the side of his house. He might be placed on his side, on his back, or in a seated position with the knees pulled up close to the chest. Cremation was common in some areas, especially in the Northern Lowlands of Yucatán. Many burials were in clay pots, the bodies within having been drawn up in a flexed position.

During Classic times the pattern of settlement in Maya com-munities was a dispersed one. Houses were built around compounds that may have housed large family units, and these units were grouped into small villages of 100 to 150 persons. Villages were the nuclei of peasant activity, including marketing, religious affairs, and social life.

From available evidence we can gain some idea of the lifeways of the Maya. Village and town activities may have been directed by subchiefs who were in communication with the rulers at the capital city. Beyond the capital city Tikal land was probably com-munal. The subchiefs directed agricultural activities, including con-struction of raised fields, canals, reservoirs, and terraces. Other subchiefs directed the system of milpa farming. This agricultural practice consisted of clearing the forest of trees by cutting and burning, planting the seed, weeding, and harvesting. Slash-and-burn farming was necessary because of the lack of draft animals to till the soil with plows. A family would farm one area for a period of four to eight years, depending on the richness of the soil, and then seek a new forest area for cultivation.

Guatemalan archaeologists have continued the work of restoration of Tikal since the University of Pennsylvania project ended. The area of the Plaza of the Seven Temples has been cleared, and one structure has been restored. Restoration has also continued at the Palace of Windows (formerly called the Bat Palace) and at Group G. More recently the Lost World Pyramid (Late Preclassic Period) and the adjacent plaza area have been restored. This section of the Tikal ceremonial center is west of the Plaza of the Seven Temples. Future years should see many more structures restored in this great ceremonial center.

A walk on any of the jungle trails surrounding Tikal can be a startling experience. Jaguars still lurk in the forest, iguanas rustle in the dry leaves, and an occasional snake can be seen slipping away into a wet ravine. Moving in a single line, an army of leaf-cutter ants journeys over miniature trails on the jungle floor. The forest is a haven for strange-sounding insects, exotic birds, and other creatures. Showers of yellow flowers drop from the tall palo-blanco trees. Occasionally an amapola tree, with brilliant orange blossoms, can be seen on the distant horizon. Mahogany, chicle, and cedar are the dominant trees in the forest. These are often covered with countless varieties of tropical vines and strangling figs. The scent of the allspice bush permeates the air when the leaves are crushed underfoot. Orchids, ferns, bromeliads, and other epiphytes hang from the damp limbs of trees. This is the forest of Petén that the Maya conquered and cultivated and in which they built their great city with its many pyramids thrusting toward the sky. It was here that a great trade center was established for the distribution of goods to other cities throughout the vast countryside. Tikal was the largest of the Maya cities and may have served as a capital for a part of the Central Lowland area during Late Classic time. The cultural decline of the Maya in the Terminal Classic (A.D. 800-900) meant the gradual abandonment of the city, and in the ensuing centuries the forest smothered the city, hiding it from the outside world.

4   The Motagua River Basin: Copán and Quiriguá

Copán

A country road winds from the village of San José de Copán to a fertile valley, across a stream used by the townfolk to wash their clothes during the cool hours of the morning, through the tobacco fields, and past the small airstrip adjacent to the ruins of the archaeological zone Copán. The approach to the ruins is through a thicket of trees where many old mounds are seen still to be uncovered by the archaeologists. A pathway through the woods leads to the Great Plaza. The first view of the ruins is breathtaking as one gazes over the acres of courts and plazas surrounded by buildings and studded with heroic sculptured monuments. As many as 10,000 persons may have lived here during the Late Classic Period, when they were exporting their distinctive Copador pottery.

Ceremonial centers such as Copán were the focal point for the Maya, but here is a ceremonial center unlike any other. At Copán one does not see great palaces with roof combs or intricate façades, nor the high pyramids conspicuous at other Maya sites. The regional difference in sculpture and architecture is immediately apparent: the Copán Maya created a ceremonial center that is unparalleled in its architectural beauty. There is restraint in the height of the buildings. Emphasis is on horizontal planes broken by monumental sculptures, a plan that establishes a sense of human scale and acts as a unifying force to the plaza. Around the Great Plaza bands of stairways covering several acres and encircling it on three sides create a quiet, sustained dignity. The architects who planned Copán wanted it to be distinctive, unlike any other Maya city, and the design for this ceremonial center was meant to be impressive. The expansive plaza, with its many flamboyant stelae and so-called altars; the ball court, a Maya classic with its associated low build-

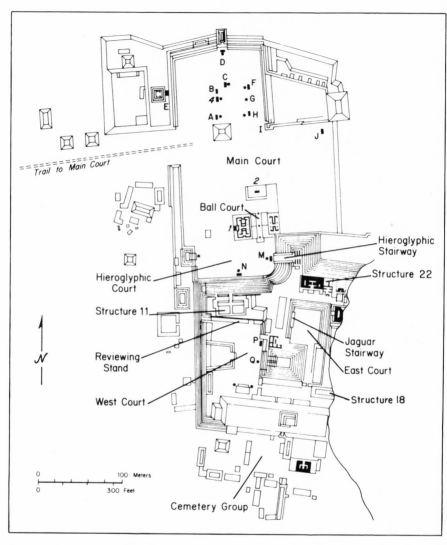

Copán. After Morley.

ings; the Hieroglyphic Court, a spectacular amphitheater for pageants; and the great palacelike structures leading to the East and West courts at the southern end of the Acropolis—all of these must have been overwhelming to the casual visitor of the day. Toward the east from the ceremonial center is a *sacbé*, or causeway, one kilometer long, leading to a residential area.

To understand the artists and craftsmen working at this time, to grasp the differences between Copán and other Maya cities, and to appreciate just how the various sections of this ceremonial center functioned, we must examine each part of the center and gain a comprehensive view of the whole.

The Great Plaza is distinguished by the presence of some of the most important stelae and altars in the area. Visually abounding with open space, the plaza was clearly designed for the majestic ceremonies that were an intrinsic part of the Maya lifeways. Murals at Uaxactún and Bonampak, as well as pottery depicting ceremonial scenes, provide some information on ceremonial life in other Maya areas, and we can assume that it was similar here. Elaborate ceremonies seem to have been required to appease the gods at crucial times in the life of the Maya. The planting and harvesting season certainly required ceremonies. Great pomp and pageantry were essential at the time when rule was transferred from father to son. The appointment of officials to high posts in the Maya hierarchy demanded ceremonies, and there were also rituals associated with death, childbirth, and marriage. For many of these occasions the populace may have been invited to participate. The ceremonies in connection with the great Maya sport, the ball game, were especially noteworthy. Since the Maya at Copán were great astronomers and astrologers, ceremonies were also performed to mark important events in the Maya calendar. It was at times such as these that stelae, altars, and buildings were dedicated.

At one time the floor of the Great Plaza was plastered and painted. Today it is kept as a green lawn dotted with twelve stelae. Many more are scattered throughout the ruins; some are in the distant hills and along the roadside. There are more skillfully carved stelae at Copán than at any other Maya site. These stelae are vertical stone monuments, approximately ten to twelve feet high, on

Detail of the head of Stela C, at Copán. The original red paint, commonly used on stelae throughout the Maya area, can still be seen. The color was preserved because the stela fell over, face down, many centuries ago and thus escaped weathering. The figure portrays a Maya ruler in Late Classic times.

which are carved full-figure portraits of rulers or other important persons of the time. The so-called ceremonial bars that they hold in their arms may have been scepters of authority. The carving is in such high relief that some of the figures are nearly in the round. The typical Copán stela carving is found nowhere else except Toniná, which has only inferior examples, and Palenque, which has only one stela. The sides or backs of Copán stelae have hieroglyphs that record specific time sequences, historical events such as dynastic succession, and other data, much of which is yet to be deciphered.

At Copán the stone used by the carvers was a greenish-col-

The east face of Stela C depicts a man more youthful than the one portrayed on the west side. The stela is dated A.D. 782. In the distance is Stela B.

Stela A, dated A.D. 731, in the Great Plaza. The face is among the more sensitively carved portraits at Copán. All the figures on stelae here obviously portray dynastic rulers or the highest aristocrats of Maya society. This stela bears the emblem glyphs for four primary centers: Copán, Tikal, Calakmul(?), and Palenque.

This noble portrait on Stela B, at Copán, shows a ruler with a goatee, a popular fashion of the time. Goatees are also seen on figures at Quiriguá, a site nearby. The diadem crowning the headdress may have been made of shell.

The back and sides of Stela A, at Copán, carved in beautifully executed glyphs. In the right columns are emblem glyphs for four major Maya cities. Stelae at Copán rest over small cruciform chambers that at one time contained caches. The chamber below Stela A has been left exposed so that visitors can study its construction.

ored andesite. The stone is ideal for carving because of its generally fine texture and even grain, and the quarry is less than a mile away, just over a hill on the way to the village. The only disadvantage of this stone is that occasionally very hard, flintlike concretions shaped like cannonballs protrude from it. Where these concretions appeared, the Maya craftsmen had to use their ingenuity. Several solutions were adopted. At one time or another the carvers incorporated the hard nodules into the overall design; allowed them to protrude, interrupting the design; cut them out, leaving hollows; or ground them down. This last task was arduous and very time-consuming. Using on these monuments only stone, bone, or wooden tools, the sculptors achieved remarkable results.

The color and texture of aged stone can be beautiful. Andesite is especially appealing, for the many centuries of exposure to the sun have bleached it somewhat. Blue-gray lichens and yellow-to-orange algae also add color to some of the stones. As mentioned earlier, during the time of Maya rule the plazas, courts, sculptures, and buildings were plastered and painted in various colors, red and blue being dominant. Traces of red can still be seen on some of the stelae. In the Great Plaza, Stela C (A.D. 782) bears especially conspicuous weathered blotches of red paint. This particular monument fell to the ground many centuries ago, so that the color was not exposed to extreme weathering. When Copán was reconstructed by the Carnegie Institution in 1934, Stela C was placed in its original upright position. This monument is the only one in the Great Plaza with two full standing figures; one faces east, and the other west. There is another double-figured stela in the Hieroglyphic Court, Stela N, dated A.D. 761.

Of the many portrayals of dignitaries on the stelae a few have especially handsome, sensitive faces, attesting to the individual sculptor's skill and creative imagination. Three faces of particular note are that of a most imposing man with a complete beard, carved on the west side of Stela C; that of the very Oriental-looking person on Stela B (A.D. 731), wearing a Mandarin-like headdress; and that on Stela A (also dated 731), a face as sensuous as any great master could carve. The important aristocrats on these monuments are Copán rulers clothed in the most resplendent garments and decorated with precious jade pieces and brilliant feathers of rare, exotic birds. Their regal headdresses are enhanced by the addition of elaborate masklike forms and zoomorphic creatures, symbols with religious significance. Much of the regalia on the headdresses may have been worn only by specific high-ranking persons. Zoomorphic forms were associated with certain priests or deities. On some of the stelae decorations that probably represent iridescent blue-green quetzal feathers, adorned with jade buttons and tassels, extend from the headdress of the personage to the feet. Most of these dignitaries are laden with anklets, bracelets, earplugs, and pendants of jade. The usual dress is a breechcloth, but one person is shown wearing a jaguar-skin skirt (see below). The figures wear various styles of sandals, some with high backs. The realistic portraits on these monuments are in marked contrast to the highly stylized faces seen at most other sites. Apparently the Copán artists were not influenced to any great degree by the more northern Maya cultures.

Among the many impressive monuments in the Great Plaza, some are especially worthy of mention. The glyphs on the back of Stela A are as fine a carving as one can see at Copán. The glyph forms on this monument are made up of animal figures, human heads, and many abstract symbols. On one side of Stela A are the emblem glyphs for four primary centers: Tikal, Copán, Palenque, and (perhaps) Calakmul. Stela A is dated A.D. 731. Another important monument, Stela H (A.D. 782), has been the subject of debate among archaeologists. Over the years many archaeologists have asserted that the figure portrays a woman (possibly a woman ruler), because of the attire worn: a jaguar-skin skirt and an apron of jade beads. Recently that identification has been questioned by noted scholars. For the Maya the skirt-type dress was characteristic of either a man or a woman. This same kind of dress can be seen on one of the figures on the stucco-sculptured pillars supporting the façade of the Temple of the Inscriptions in Palenque.

Stela D (A.D. 736), at the extreme north end of the plaza, has particular significance because of the full-figure glyphs carved on the back of the monument. Full-figure glyphs are a rarely used variant for numerals. The Maya used three systems of symbols for

Detail of a glyph on Stela A, Copán, shows the encrustation of lichens and algae accumulated over the years. The affixes to the glyph are readily noticeable.

numerals from 1 to 19: a system of dots and bars, human-head glyphs, and full-figure glyphs. Here at Copán the full-figure glyph can also be seen on the facing of the top step of the Hieroglyphic Stairway, and on Altar 41, the double-headed zoomorphic altar in the west end of the Hieroglyphic Court. On Stela D can be seen the Copán emblem glyph, a leaf-nosed bat. It can be seen on Stela A as well. Other sites having full-figure glyphs are Quiriguá, Yaxchilán, and Palenque.

Under each stela at Copán is a small cruciform chamber. In one arm of these chambers have been found caches of miscellaneous objects, including obsidian blades, pottery, and other simple objects

Stela D overlooks the Great Plaza at Copán. This plaza was at one time plastered and painted. The inscription on the back of Stela D has full-figure glyphs. The stela is dated A.D. 736. A zoomorphic altar stands in front of the stela.

Stela H, Copán, depicts a ruler in full ceremonial dress: a jaguar-skin skirt with a jade or bone apron crisscrossed over it. This particular kind of dress is often seen at Palenque. Skirts of this style, both long and short, were worn by both men and women. Stela H was dedicated in A.D. 782.

The Great Plaza at Copán is studded with beautifully carved stelae and altars. In the foreground is Altar G, the monument of latest date at Copán, A.D. 800. The unusual shape of the altar is that of a double-headed serpent with human heads emerging from its jaws. In the distance is Stela H.

used as offerings. Cruciform chambers under stelae are found only at Copán.

Each stela faces a low, flat monument that we have called an "altar." Altars may be round, square, or of irregular shape. As yet we do not know for what purpose the Maya used these monuments. Their shapes give us no particular guidance. Some of them may in fact have been altars, but there is no conclusive proof that they were. Most religions have altars at which offerings are made to the gods. Since the Maya religion has a pantheon of gods, many kinds of offerings would have been made, in different ways and by different societal groups. Even today the Maya in remote regions of the countryside practice their older religion by leaving offerings to their gods. These remote shrines and altars are on mountainsides and in cornfields, far from the touring public. Another purpose for the altars at Copán surely must have been as commemorative monuments like the stelae.

The altar in front of Stela D is typical of many: a grotesque zoomorphic form with two heads. Zoomorphic monuments may be combinations of several animals, such as serpents, turtles, jaguars, and frogs. Human features, such as human heads in the open jaws of serpents, may be incorporated as well. On some of the altars it is no easy matter to tell exactly what animals the sculptors were trying to represent. It would seem that their attitude in regard to the animals on monuments was influenced more by religious needs and social aspirations than by a wish to represent a given animal realistically. Quiriguá, just thirty miles from the Copán ceremonial center, is especially noted for large zoomorphic monuments.

Adjacent to Stela C is one of the most peculiar of the altars at Copán. A shallow circular pond was made of stone and stuccoed, and a very large sculptured turtle was placed in it. The head and legs were carved separately, giving it the appearance of mobility. Zoomorphic sculptures such as these added variety to the monuments in this Great Plaza.

Near Stela H is a group of three altars representing serpents. Two of the altars are identical: double-headed feathered serpents with arched backs. The third altar (Altar G) is also in the shape of a double-headed serpent whose jaws hold human heads. On the south side of this altar is carved the date in glyphs corresponding to A.D. 800—the latest date carved on a monument at Copán. Shortly after that date Copán went into a cultural decline and was later abandoned. Tropical growth encroached on the ruins until the nineteenth century when John Lloyd Stephens, the American explorer-adventurer, discovered the site.

There is a tendency for American Indians to be stereotyped as beardless. This is not wholly accurate; many American Indian men can and do grow beards. Beards must have been fashionable during the Classic Period at Copán, for the figures on Stelae B and D have goatees, the figure on Stela C has a full beard, and that on Stela F has a moustache. The faces missing from several

The west face of Stela C, at Copán. Another full standing ruler appears on the east face. The depiction of two full figures on one stela is unusual. The ruler portrayed on the west face is the only full-bearded figure at Copán; there are, however, several faces with goatees. A turtle altar stands in front of the stela (A.D. 782).

other stelae may also have had beards. Soon after this time beards became fashionable on stelae at Quiriguá. The Olmecs in Veracruz carved monuments with bearded persons more than a thousand years before the Classic Period. All manner of beards, goatees, sideburns, and moustaches are seen on sculptures at Palenque.

The eighth century was the Golden Age of the Maya at Copán, and most of the sculpture and architecture at the site today is of that period. The preceding century was a vigorous one, however, not to be underestimated in terms of productivity and artistic ability. Dating from this earlier period are two stelae in the Great Plaza, one in the West Court, and others scattered farther from the main

The back of Stela F, at Copán, has a unique rope design entwining five blocks of glyphs. Feathers arranged with buttons, part of the dress of the ruler shown on the opposite side of the stela, sweep around the back of the monument, creating a pleasant pattern. The beautifully carved glyphs date the stela A.D. 721.

Stela J was the first monument carved after the Great Plaza at Copán was completed in A.D. *702. The stela is dated* A.D. *707. The basket-weave design for the pattern of the glyphs is unique at Copán, although a similar stela (Monument 8) was carved at Quiriguá in* A.D. *751.*

site. These earlier figures have a decided somberness and stiffness. The sculptors had not yet freed their figures and costumes from the massive block of stone. The relief carving is not deep; the feet face outward, parallel to the front of the figures; and the carving has a slightly archaic look. During the next one hundred years stelae figures gradually changed. The feet were carved farther forward as each decade passed until they reached a forty-five-degree angle. Clothing became more ornate, and the arms and legs of the figures more realistic. On Stela 4 (A.D. 783) the legs are carved in the round to such a degree that they are nearly freed from the monument. As the garments, along with methods of carving them, became more complicated, a baroque style emerged that was at times ponderous. In the evolving style of the stelae we are aware of the cultural flowering of a people working within the framework of their tradition and with respect for the experience of four centuries of previous sculptural achievements.

Stela N (A.D. 761), at the base of the Great Stairway to Temple 11, has the only filigree stone carving at Copán. For the figure on each side the sculptor carved an elaborate headdress nearly as large as the figure. The pedestal on which Stela N is erected is the only one at Copán with hieroglyphic inscriptions.

The degree to which Copán influenced other cultural centers in Honduras, Guatemala, and groups much farther south has yet to be determined. Quiriguá, the neighboring site, is a case in point. Like all the other Maya cultural centers Quiriguá created its own regional style. An exception to this is Stela H (A.D. 751). On this monument the artist arranged his hieroglyphs in a basket-weave pattern. There is only one other stela similar to it, and that is Stela J (A.D. 702) at Copán, carved exactly forty-four years earlier. Quiriguá was not a great center, but it is an interesting site. From all indications the area was not heavily populated, and the ceremonial center is small, with few large structures. However, its sculptors were highly skilled in carving. It seems quite possible that Quiriguá may have been controlled or dominated for a time by Copán. Recent hieroglyphic research by David Kelley indicates a possible marriage alliance between Copán and Quiriguá. Another inscription tells of the capture of Copán's ruler, 18 Rabbit, by a

The Ball Court at Copán is considered to be one of the best-proportioned courts in the area. The six parrot heads tenoned into the benches may have served as markers. Late Classic.

lord of Quiriguá in A.D. 737. Artists from Copán may have been employed at Quiriguá to carve some of the monuments during its early history.

Next to the Great Plaza at Copán is the area intended for the most famous of all sports in Mesoamerica, the ball game. The Copán Ball Court (A.D. 775) is considered a classic in proportions, even though it is quite small. The court is in the shape of an I with buildings on either side. They may have been dressing rooms in which the players donned the ceremonial regalia that was a festive part of the ball game. One of the chambers in the buildings may have been used by the priests as a place to appease the gods. A third possible use would be as an area for visiting dignitaries to pass the time before the start of the game. Along the center of each sidewall of the Ball Court are benches with hieroglyphic inscriptions from top to bottom. It would appear that the Copán Maya were greatly preoccupied with recording data on buildings, and the Ball Court was no exception.

Excavations revealed two additional ball courts under this one, the earliest dating from the second century A.D. Immediately under the present court were circular stone markers carved in low relief, depicting players of the ball game in action. These markers, as well as other artifacts from Copán, have been removed to the little museum in the village. The existing three markers running down the middle of the court are square. Markers may have been used to score the game or to indicate boundaries.

Our only source of information on how the game was played is the Spanish account of the Aztec game by Fray Diego Durán, an account recorded more than six hundred years after Copán ceased to be active. The Aztec game was played by two teams, each with three to nine players. A hard rubber ball weighing six

The Hieroglyphic Stairway at Copán has the longest single inscription found to date. Glyphs, approximately twenty-five hundred in all, are carved on the facings of each step. The stairway is studded with five heroic figures, one of which was removed to the Peabody Museum, in Cambridge, Massachusetts.

or seven pounds was used. Much smaller balls (approximately three inches in diameter) were used at Dainzú in the Oaxaca Valley, and smaller balls may also have been used by the Maya in some kinds of games. The object of the game was to keep the ball from hitting the floor of the court while the teams tried to score. Because of the rough-and-tumble action of the game the players' knees, elbows, loins, and waists were padded. The ball could be hit only with the elbow, knee, or hip. From the design of the courts, probably the ways of scoring and playing the game changed many times over the centuries. Needless to say, the Maya must have participated in innumerable kinds of ball games, and most ceremonial centers had several courts. Recently a second ball court at Copán, much smaller than the court in the Great Plaza, has been excavated and reconstructed. It lies southwest of the West Court of the main ceremonial center.

Six tenoned parrot heads are sunk into the slanting benches of the side walls of the court. The same kind of head also has been found at La Unión, just a few miles southeast of Copán, and at Asunción Mita, in Guatemala near the El Salvador border.

As viewed from the Ball Court, the importance of the Hieroglyphic Stairway leading to Temple 26 becomes apparent. A delicately controlled and sophisticated style prevails as one's gaze moves toward the top. The facings on the sixty-three steps are carved with approximately 2,500 glyphs, the longest known Maya inscription. Historical data here span the time period from A.D. 544 to 744. At five intervals in the center of the stairs are splendid heroic six-foot-high figures seated on thrones. The most handsome figure of the group was removed many years ago to the Peabody Museum, in Cambridge, Massachusetts. The Hieroglyphic Stairway should aid in the deciphering of many Maya glyphs in the years to come.

On either side of the stairway a balustrade runs to the top, carved with celestial bird and serpent motifs. In marked contrast to the realism of the heroic figures, the balustrades are worked in an abstract design that leaves the animals' identity in some question. Some are clearly serpents, which are generously depicted on stairways throughout Mesoamerica. The sculptors of most of the

This large head is believed to have been a part of the cornice of Temple 11, at Copán. Larger than life size, the carving shows an unusual human quality in the facial expression.

important Classic cities as well as those of the Postclassic phase adapted the serpent to a variety of innovative art styles. The serpent was the most important animal for decorative detail, perhaps because its undulating body lent itself particularly well to designs for many architectural details. Aside from this, the serpent was important in Maya mythology and as a fertility deity, as depicted on vases and in murals.

Since earthquakes and tree roots had crumbled most of the steps, the task of reconstruction was like trying to put together a jigsaw puzzle with many pieces missing. Stela M, at the base of the Hieroglyphic Stairway, records a solar eclipse, showing the Maya's astonishing scientific awareness for that time. The date of the stela is A.D. 756.

Looking at the Ball Court with its associated buildings, the adjoining Hieroglyphic Court with the famous Hieroglyphic Stairway, and, toward the north, the Great Stairway leading to Temple 11, we become aware of the conscious design of the Copán architects that achieved relationship and unity among the various buildings, stairways, and sculptured forms.

At right angles to the Hieroglyphic Stairway is the Great Stairway to Temple 11, which was inaugurated in the year A.D. 763. This stairway acts as a divider between the northern and southern parts of the Acropolis. On the south is the West Court, an enclosure of nearly an acre that gives the intimate feeling of a much smaller court. Stela P (A.D. 623) and at least three altars dating from an earlier period must have been brought into this court from another area after it was constructed. The practice of using older monuments in this way is also evident at Tikal. However, there were times in Tikal's history when the monuments were destroyed or defaced. At Copán this was never a practice. Stela E (A.D. 616) and Stela I (A.D. 677) are also from the earlier period. These stelae are in the main court.

The Reviewing Stand on the north side of the West Court is an imposing edifice with a stairway fifty feet long leading to Temple 11. At the top of the stairs, on the extreme sides, are two large kneeling torchbearing figures with snakes in their mouths and around their waists. Three enormous conch shells are placed be-

On the stairway of the Reviewing Stand in the West Court at Copán are two grotesque figures holding what may be torches. Serpents writhe around the waists and necks and through the mouths of these unusual figures.

tween these grotesque figures. In the wall behind these sculptural pieces are ten large niches, two having connecting rooms. They may have been used to hold objects used during festivals, ceremonies, or commemorative events. The height of this platform and stairway suggests its possible use as a staging area for the pageantry that took place in the West Court.

The West Court is noted for the sculptured figures on Altar Q, at the base of Pyramid 16. Carved in A.D. 776, the altar was once believed to have been dedicated to the lunar cycle. The most recent analysis of Altar Q, however, repudiates the old astronomical theory and suggests that the monument was dedicated to the

Altar Q, in the West Court, stands near the highest mound in Copán. The top of the altar is carved in glyphs, and around the sides are sixteen persons seated on cushions with glyphs.

None of their headdresses are alike. The altar was dedicated in A.D. *776 and is believed to record the accession of the young ruler Yax Macaw to the throne.*

young ruler Yax Macaw (New Sun-at-Horizon) on his accession to the throne. The top of this altar is sculptured in blocks of hieroglyphs. On each of the four sides of the altar are seated figures, sixteen in all, dressed in similar clothes. All are seated on cushions carved with glyphs. All the figures are facing the west side of the altar, where the two central personages face each other as if in a commemorative gesture. They hold in their hands what may be emblems of office. Between the two figures is the date A.D. 763. Similar to these figures are rows of carved seated figures that were on the inner steps of the Temple of the Inscriptions (Structure 11). These sculptures are now in the British Museum.

Sculptures showing human figures seated cross-legged are rare at Copán. Other than those on Altar Q, the only seated figures are those on the back of Stela B and on the top of either side of Stela N. Seated figures are more commonly depicted at Piedras Negras, Yaxchilán, and Palenque, and they also frequently occur on ceramics of the Late Classic Period (A.D. 600–900). The Bonampak murals are well illustrated with figures in this particular pose. A seated figure very similar to the figures on Altar Q appears at a distant northern site, Xochicalco, near Cuernavaca. Instances of the influence of the Maya on other cultures as far north as this, and as far south as the Nicoya Peninsula in Costa Rica, are not uncommon.

Walking toward the East Court, one sees an opening through the trees, revealing the Copán River in the valley far below. This river had been eating into the bank of the Acropolis for many centuries, and as a result sections of the East Court fell to their destruction during landslides. One of the first major tasks in reconstructing Copán was to divert the course of the river, thus avoiding further catastrophe, a project that took two years. Along this area of the riverbank are many mounds still waiting to be investigated.

Most Maya ceremonial centers have characteristics in common. They have stepped pyramids crowned with temples that face onto a central quadrangular plaza, palaces and ceremonial buildings clustered around smaller courtyards, platforms with flanking stairways as approaches to the buildings, and stelae and altars as com-

Heroic jaguar on the wall of the Jaguar Stairway in the East Court. At one time disks of obsidian were inserted for the animal's spots. Because of the importance of Temple 22, the East Court may well have been the most important court at Copán.

memorative monuments. There are considerable regional differences, however, in the construction, stylistic evolution, and functions of ceremonial centers.

The most important court at Copán may have been the East Court. Here the architecture is distinguished by a harmony of proportion and by a decorative detail that is not only impressive but imaginative. On the west side of the court is the Jaguar Stairway,

Little remains of Temple 22 at Copán but the walls and the beautiful portal door sculptured in high relief. The door is decorated with a double-headed serpent arranged over the top and down the sides. Its heads rest on Atlantean figures kneeling on skulls. This magnificent temple is believed to have been dedicated to the planet Venus.

a unique contribution to the architecture of Copán. Two mighty jaguars as tall as men stand in most dramatic poses on either end of this stairway. These animals were carved to receive inlays of obsidian for the spots on their bodies. In the center of the staircase is an equally original sculpture—the great rectangular Venus mask, also carved in very high relief. Like the Reviewing Stand in the West Court, the Jaguar Stairway may have been used for watching ceremonial activities associated with the court. At times architecture such as that exemplified here provides us with some understanding of the patterns of human behavior in a country where humidity has destroyed most other kinds of documentary evidence.

Facing to the north of the East Court, another magnificent stairway leads to the most important temple building in Copán, Temple 22, dedicated in A.D. 765. Here is one of the finest carved stone doorways to be seen in the Maya world. A baroque decoration consisting of a carved two-headed serpent borders the doorway. Each end of the serpent is held up by an Atlantean kneeling figure resting on a skull. In marked contrast to the portal door is the serenity of the plain façade of the temple.

Traces of the original color can still be seen on the interior walls. As many as twenty-five coatings of plaster have been detected on the exterior of the building. The Maya plastered and repainted their buildings periodically, usually to coincide with a five-, ten-, or twenty-year cycle. These cycles were important commemorative times for erecting new buildings, stelae, and altars and for rededicating monuments to the gods and ruling chiefs. This particular temple is believed to have been dedicated to the planet Venus.

The whole platform adjoining Temple 22 is a glorious place from which to view the north end of the ceremonial center. In the late afternoon sun the courts are in deep shadows, and the Hieroglyphic Stairway sparkles in the warm glow of the filtered light. Large ceiba trees, deeply rooted in the ruins, drape their branches over the sides of the temple walls like ghosts from the past.

On the tip of the south end of the East Court, overlooking the Copán River, is the newly restored Structure 18, a small but significant edifice with several panels of reliefs.

On one of the grassy banks of the road leading back to the village are two large stelae facing the evening sun. These monuments are a part of an earlier period in Copán than that of the Acropolis. The powerful-looking ruling chief carved on Stela 6 (A.D. 683) stands here as though witnessing the conquests of future generations. Stela 5 nearby has a panel of twenty glyphs and a

Stela 6 stands beside the road leading from the village of Copán to the archaeological zone. It was dedicated in A.D. 682, just a few years before the completion of the Great Plaza at Copán. A number of stelae are outside the main archaeological zone. This massive heroic figure shows the more static style of sculpture that had evolved by the end of the seventh century.

Throughout the ruins at Copán are sculptures on the sides of walls and mounds, but they are not in situ. These two heads suggest the kind of decoration that the Maya enjoyed on their buildings.

carved human figure with the date A.D. 706.

All evidence from archaeological findings indicates that Copán was a major Maya city during the Late Classic Period, but there is also evidence of occupation during Preclassic and Early Classic times. The ceremonial center of Copán is only a small part of the total array of structures in the Copán region. Many residential areas, some for the elite and others for those of lower status, are situated along the Copán River valley, extending from the main ceremonial center. Copán influenced towns and villages along the Motagua and Ulua rivers, which drain into the Caribbean, and the Pacific coastal areas from El Salvador down to Costa Rica. Many

109

of the discoveries in astronomy and the refinements in the arts influenced other Maya cultural areas on the north and other cultures in the Mexican highlands. The contribution that the Maya scientists, architects, and artists of Copán bequeathed to the rest of mankind is one that only a great civilization could have produced.

Quiriguá

The mist always seems to be present at Quiriguá. Even when the sun breaks through, only moments later another shower sweeps the rain forest, spreading a rainbow across the moss-laden ruins. The Motagua River separates this rain forest area from the rich fertile valleys toward the south, where the ceremonial city of Copán is located. Flowing north to the Caribbean Sea, the Motagua River parallels the northern boundary between Guatemala and Honduras. One of the sources of Maya jade was the Motagua River bed. Here jade boulders, smaller stones, and pebbles were ground smooth by the constant churn of the river current. It is possible that the two-hundred-pound jade boulder found at Kaminaljuyú, in Guatemala City, was from the Motagua River. Other riverbeds, however, as well as the Guatemala Highlands, also yielded jade. Quiriguá may have gained its importance in Late Classic times by controlling the jade and obsidian markets, as well as the trade routes along the Motagua River.

For many years the ruins of Quiriguá, along with thousands of acres of banana plantations in the surrounding country, were owned by the United Fruit Company. Most of this property is now owned or controlled by the Guatemala government. The large hospital that was once maintained by the United Fruit Company now lies in ruin. In past years many a weary traveler wishing to see the Quiriguá site was graciously housed here for the night. Until 1970 a two-mile hike along the railroad track from the small village of Quiriguá was the only approach to the ruins. Now a road has been cut through to the area so that it is accessible by car.

The ceremonial center of Quiriguá is not a large one, but we do not know how large was the residential area that surrounded

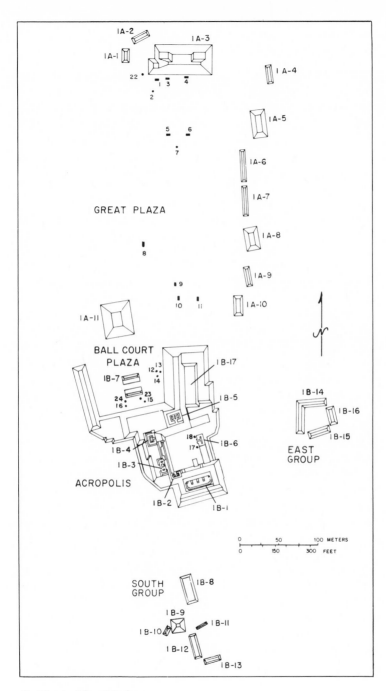

Quiriguá. After Morley.

the center. It is apparent from recent research that a large populace lived in the rich agricultural countryside and that villages,
possibly controlled by Quiriguá, extended along the Motagua River
toward the Caribbean. The whole visible site is no more than ten
acres. When the United Fruit Company bought the area in 1909
for its plantations, it set aside thirty acres for the archaeological
zone, leaving untouched the magnificent virgin forest surrounding
the site. Since the rain forest has not been cut back sufficiently
from the ruins, the constant dampness has meant that most of the
monuments and buildings are covered with moss and lichens, and
the buildings are overgrown with the constantly encroaching jungle.

Quiriguá was unknown to the outside world until its discovery
by John Lloyd Stephens and Frederick Catherwood in 1840. Shortly
after this the English archaeologist Alfred Maudslay spent some
time at the site, and the world is greatly indebted to him for his
superb, finely executed drawings of the stelae and zoomorphs. Excavations were carried out by Edgar L. Hewett and Sylvanus G.
Morley in 1910, at which time some restoration of two buildings
was begun. The ceremonial site of Quiriguá had been abandoned
over a thousand years before, and during the passage of time many
trees had fallen, knocking down monuments and crushing buildings.
In 1934 the United Fruit Company engaged E. H. Morris and
Gustav Stromsvik to reconstruct broken monuments and reerect
several that had toppled over. In 1975 the University of Pennsylvania and the government of Guatemala joined forces to excavate
and restore more extensively the Quiriguá ceremonial center.

The first glimpse of the ruins reveals the Great Plaza. This
plaza and the Acropolis south of it are the only cleared areas at
Quiriguá. Jungle paths lead to excavated foundations; other ruins
are still covered with the tropical-forest growth. From the Great
Plaza the most that can be seen is the series of stately stelae and
zoomorphic monuments which command the attention of all who
visit here. Large mounds covering ancient ruins yet to be excavated
stand all around the Great Plaza, well hidden by a mantle of green
vegetation.

Even though Quiriguá is a very small ceremonial center, it is
marked by many unique features. The sculptors here created the

tallest monolithic monuments and carved the largest zoomorphic monuments in the Maya world. The style of these heroic monuments, as well as that of the many other sculptures in Quiriguá, is in marked contrast to the flamboyant style of Copán.

It would be difficult to believe that Quiriguá could have been completely independent of Copán. The two cities are only thirty miles apart, and they flourished at the same time, reaching a great artistic climax during the Late Classic Period (A.D. 600–900). In the light of recent glyphic research it is probable that the ruling families at Quiriguá were related to those at Copán. David Kelley, who has made a genetic study of the hieroglyphics at Quiriguá and Copán, traces Quiriguá dynastic rule for five successive ruling families over a period of seventy-five years. Further study of the glyphs may give us a deeper insight into the nature of Maya history in this region and the relationship of Quiriguá with other Maya cities and towns.

Pottery and fragments of figurines found at Quiriguá indicate that the area was occupied in the Late Preclassic Period. During the Early Classic, Southern Lowland Maya probably moved into the area as colonists. The monuments and structures we see today, however, are from the Late Classic Period. The history of Quiriguá really begins at a site near the old United Fruit Company hospital, about two miles from the present ceremonial center. At this early location are two stelae and a single temple. At a second center not far from this one another stela was erected. A third center ultimately became the final site, with greatly increased activity and artistic production. The two earliest monuments (20 and 21), with glyphs dating from the latter part of the fifth century, stand in Group A on a ridge near the present ceremonial center. All the monuments in the main ceremonial center are Late Classic.

Upon entering the archaeological zone, one sees immediately the five tallest stelae. Monuments 1, 3, and 4 are in a line running from east to west. Just beyond these are the two tallest monuments, 5 and 6. The subject matter on the stelae at Quiriguá is the same as that on the stelae at Copán. A standing ruler dominates one or both sides of each monument, and descriptive glyphs are arranged to fill most of the remaining space. In many ways

113

the attitudes of the figures on the various monuments, as well as their dress, are much the same. Sculptures at Quiriguá, however, lack the variety of form and the three-dimensional quality of the sculptures found at Copán. The faces of the dignitaries on sculptures at Quiriguá likewise lack the sensitive individual expression noted at Copán. One of the longest reigns at Quiriguá was that of Cauac Sky, inaugurated in A.D. 724, who ruled for over fifty years and was responsible for expanding the ceremonial center and for adding many of the monuments in the Great Plaza. Monument 5 bears two heroic portrayals of this ruler, one on each side. He is represented on six other monuments (Monuments 1, 3, 4, 6, 8, and 10), with text pertaining to his reign. Monument 7 records his death in 784. In 737 he captured 18 Rabbit, ruler of Copán. Quiriguá's independence from Copán may have followed this date. The last ruler of Quiriguá, Jade Sky, is portrayed on Monument 11.

There are some peculiarities on Quiriguá stelae. The proportion of most figures is dwarfed by tall headdresses. The ceremonial bar signifying the staff of office as used at Copán is replaced on most stelae at Quiriguá by the Manikin Scepter. The scepter, held diagonally in the right hand, consists of a staff with the Long-nosed God on one end and the head of a snake terminating the leg of the manikin at the other end. The Manikin Scepter was also used in Tikal in Early Classic times and is believed to have been introduced from the Highlands, possibly from Kaminaljuyú.

Another fashion of the time was the use of beards. Starting with Monument 6 (A.D. 761), beards were carved on the figures of all monuments for the next twenty-five years. Beards were the fashion thirty years earlier on stelae at Copán. Monument 6 is considered by some scholars to have the most beautifully executed glyphs at Quiriguá. The most complex and intricately carved glyphs are on Monument 2 (Zoomorph B), the large, froglike sculpture seen as one enters the archaeological zone.

The tallest monument at Quiriguá, Monument 5, which portrays Canac Sky, weighs sixty-five tons and reaches a height of thirty-five feet. The shaft of the stela was originally sunk eight and a half feet into the ground and was set in a foundation of rough-shaped stones and red clay. When Monument 5 was reset

Monument 5, at Quiriguá, is the tallest monolithic sculpture in Meso-america. Carved of sandstone, the stela is thirty-five feet high and weighs sixty-five tons. It was dedicated in A.D. *771. Portrayed is the ruler Cauac Sky.*

in an upright position in 1934, the shaft was set in a concrete block.

To quarry such a large monument and move it to the ceremonial center was a major engineering feat. The quarry for Quiriguá is approximately three miles away. Here is found a fine sandstone, close-grained, even-textured, and ideal for carving. The stone to be quarried was first undercut in the shape of a rectangular block, the length depending on the sculptor's design. At Quiriguá the natural cleavage planes of the rock were taken advantage of and skillfully used. Pressure brought to bear along the length of the undercut stone by the use of wedges and plankings would break the stone free. Freshly quarried stone is much softer than it is after it has been exposed and aged. This is also true of the limestone used at most other Maya sites.

The rough-cut stone may have been moved from the quarry to the ceremonial center with the aid of skids. In some instances log rollers may have been employed. It is possible that part of the general shaping of the sculpture was completed before the erection of the monument, which was the next engineering feat. This was probably accomplished by means of ramps made from the great hardwood trees nearby and with the use of ropes and cables that may have been operated on the principle of a pulley in the Y of tree branches. Once the stone was erected, the artist commenced the carving with the help of scaffolding.

Stelae at Quiriguá range from ten to thirty-five feet in height. The red sandstone color and the restricted design of the figures emphasize the somber, more ponderous quality of these monoliths. Because of the hardness of this sandstone, carving in very low relief delineates most of the detail of the costume. Only the part of the figure around the head is carved in very deep relief, the face being nearly in the round. In some ways this style can be likened to the stelae at Piedras Negras. Piedras Negras and Quiriguá were the only two sites that consistently erected monuments at five-year intervals rather than the ten- or twenty-year intervals more often observed at other Classic Maya cities.

The accompanying chart shows the correlation of Maya and Christian dates recorded on monuments at Quiriguá.

116

Monument Dates at Quiriguá, with Equivalent Dates Adjusted to the Christian Calendar

Monument No.	Maya Date		Equivalent Christian Date (A.D.)
8	9.16.0.0.0	2 Ahau 13 Zec	751
10	9.16.5.0.0	8 Ahau 8 Zotz	756
6	9.16.10.0.0	1 Ahau 3 Zip	761
4	9.16.15.0.0	7 Ahau 18 Pop	766
5	9.17.0.0.0	13 Ahau 18 Cumhu	771
1	9.17.5.0.0	6 Ahau 13 Kayab	775
3	9.17.5.0.0	6 Ahau 13 Kayab	775
2	9.17.10.0.0	12 Ahau 8 Pax	780
7	9.17.15.0.0	4 Ahau 3 Muan	785
15	9.18.0.0.0	11 Ahau 18 Mac	790
23	9.18.0.0.0	11 Ahau 18 Mac	790
16	9.18.5.0.0	4 Ahau 13 Ceh	795
24	9.18.5.0.0	4 Ahau 13 Ceh	795
9	9.18.10.0.0	10 Ahau 8 Zac	800
11	9.18.15.0.0	3 Ahau 3 Yax	805
Temple 1	9.19.0.0.0	9 Ahau 18 Mol	810

The stelae at Quiriguá date from A.D. 746 to 810, all within Late Classic times. The first stela erected at the present site is Monument 8, which has the glyph date A.D. 751. This is an important monument, for it shows obviously the influence of Copán. In both Stela J at Copán and Monument 8 at Quiriguá a diagonally woven mat design is used as a pattern for the placement of glyphs. The Copán stela was carved forty-four years earlier. The cruciform, chamberlike pedestal popular at Copán was not used at Quiriguá. Instead, the butt of the stela was sunk into the ground and held in position by rough-cut stones and clay.

The arrangement of the glyphs on both the altars and the stelae is carefully designed to fill the total space provided by the artist. The Maya obsession to carve every surface of monuments and altars is fully realized in the many baroque patterns on monuments here. The glyphs on Monument 4 that represent the year

117

A.D. 766 are full-figure glyphs, noted above at Copán. At Quiriguá they can also be seen on Monument 16 (Zoomorph P), better known as the "Great Turtle Altar," as well as on Monuments 2 and 17.

The origin of the stelae-altar complex is unknown. We do know that the pattern was well developed in Late Preclassic time at the Izapa site, on the Pacific Slope of southern Mexico, and at Abaj Takalik, in Guatemala. The earliest dated monument of this kind was found at Tres Zapotes, in Veracruz—Stela C, dated 31 B.C. Undated stelae and altars were created by the Olmecs as early as the Middle Preclassic times. Future excavations in the Maya area and along its perimeter may give us a better understanding of how this monumental sculpture evolved.

After the erection of Monument 5 at Quiriguá the carving of tall monuments went into a decline, and two dwarflike stelae mark the next five-year cycle. From this time on, zoomorphs and altars were the popular carved monuments, functioning like those at Copán: to commemorate the social, religious, scientific, and historical events important to the elite and their society.

The shape of zoomorphs suggests that they never could have been used as altars. Most zoomorphs at Quiriguá look like crouching monsters. Usually double-headed and of composite identity, they have the general shape of animals such as frogs, turtles, or jaguars. Realism in depicting specific animals was not necessarily a concern of the Maya artist who was sculpturing a zoomorph, and some are hard to identify. Monument 2 is certainly close to the shape of a frog, whereas Monument 3 is shaped like a jaguar. In both monuments a human head is in the animal's mouth. Glyphs are incorporated as a part of the overall design of the zoomorph. The long history of zoomorphs, first at Copán and then at Quiriguá, set the style and pattern for the Great Turtle Altar, the last and most beautifully executed zoomorph at Quiriguá. These sculptures most likely had both mythological and religious significance.

A depression in the ground along a trail south of the archaeological zone envelops Monuments 15 and 16 (Zoomorphs O and P). Monument 15 is poorly conceived aesthetically, but it has some fine carved glyphs. The Great Turtle Altar, Monument 16, is surely one of the most magnificent stones ever carved by the Maya. In the shape of a boulder, the stone is completely decorated in fairly high relief with intricate designs interlaced with human and animal forms combined with glyphic panels. Only an extraordinary artist could have created this masterful sculpture, which transcends regional differences sometimes noted in Maya sculpture. The important personage seated in the jaws of this turtle-jaguarlike animal probably represents a ruler of Quiriguá. His dress is elaborate, and his headdress is intricate and exquisite in design; he holds a Manikin Scepter in one hand, and a shield covers the other. The Great Turtle Altar, over nine feet long and seven feet high, must have been designed to be viewed from above as well as from the sides, because a large mask form covers the top. A similar mask is carved on the back of the zoomorph. These forms and many other related and unrelated designs are united by abstract curvilinear patterns and glyphs. Maya symbolism reaches its ultimate complexity in this monument. For many years this sculpture and others at Quiriguá have been covered with moss, lichens, and other plant growth, and the roots of the plants have been eating into the surface of the stone. Periodically the overgrowth has been cleaned from the sculpture. Erosion of the stone will eventually result unless a more systematic procedure is established to keep the monuments free from plant growth.

Two slab-type altars, nearly level with the ground, were discovered next to Monuments 15 and 16 in 1934 during excavations. The designs of these altarlike sculptures are similar. Carved in low relief, they depict a masked dancer in a dramatic attitude of the dance. The remaining space on these important sculptured monuments is beautifully carved with glyphs. Since these altars have been deep below the jungle floor for many centuries, both show little stone erosion. The jungle has been both destructive and kind to the handsomely carved monuments at Quiriguá.

Just south of the Great Plaza a small acropolis surrounding a central court is reached by a flanking stairway. Recent excavations here have revealed four building stages extending from the sixth to the ninth centuries. The earliest structures were made of river cobblestones. Later superimpositions covered these earlier buildings in a dressed masonry of rhyolite. In the last outburst of

building at Quiriguá, the structures were carved of sandstone.

West of the Acropolis is an unexcavated ball court very similar in shape to the court at Copán. At a later date this ball court was covered with a platform, and on the platform a free-standing wall was constructed and decorated with three large heads of the sun god Kinich Ahau. Other small structures were also built during this time.

It is interesting to note that despite the proximity of Quiriguá to Copán in Late Classic times no Copador ware, so typical of the Copán-El Salvador area, or any other elaborately painted ceremonial vessels have been found. In fact, there is little indication of great wealth at Quiriguá other than the structures and monuments. Copper bells and Plumbate pottery, however, have been found at Quiriguá, indicating Postclassic occupation after the Maya florescence. Plumbate pottery, made from a clay with a metallic iridescence, was popularly traded during Early Postclassic times, and it became for archaeologists an important aid in dating other objects found with it. Some Plumbate pottery has a shiny surface resembling glaze. A glaze, however, was never used in Mesoamerica in pre-Spanish times. These imports, along with a sculptured chacmool, link Quiriguá with seagoing trade routes and suggest that there was commercial contact with Chichén Itzá, as well as along the Pacific Coast.

Architecture at Quiriguá is confined to smaller structures, simple in form and decoration compared to the great, complex buildings at most other major ceremonial centers of the same era. The largest building is Structure 1, which may have been used as a temple or palace. The building has three doorways leading to inner chambers. The architectural style is simple but distinctive.

Monument 16 (Zoomorph P, dated A.D. *795), at Quiriguá, is considered one of the most magnificent carvings in the Americas. The great stone is often covered with a mantle of moss and lichens because of the constant dampness, but under the mantle the stone is elaborately carved in a florescent baroque manner. The drawing accompanying the photograph (after Maudslay) shows details.*

121

The façade is divided by a medial molding of hieroglyphs. Below the molding the wall is plain, but above it the wall is decorated in a fluted pattern and painted. The top step of the stairway leading to the building is decorated with glyphs, much like the stairway leading to Temple 11 in the West Court at Copán. The other excavated structures on the raised acropolis are small and may have served ceremonial purposes.

As the midday light penetrates the foliage of the mighty hardwood trees to the plaza floor, the area surrounding Quiriguá becomes a sheath of shimmering green. The trees must have been a decided asset to the Maya. Here was wood in unending quantity for the cooking fires, construction of houses, traps for animals, ceremonial decoration for festivals, and countless other uses later assigned to metal, which was not used by the Maya during Classic times. The wealth and power of Quiriguá depended on control of trade on the Montagua River.

Endowed with rich, fertile soil for agriculture in the areas surrounding the urban center of Quiriguá, tropical forests on the distant horizon, and a wealth of technical skills passed down from one generation to another, the Maya created an elaborate ceremonial center in this rain forest that has had no equal since Classic times.

5   The Lower Usumacinta River: Palenque, Yaxchilán, and Bonampak

Palenque

The moist, palm-studded plains stretch from the Tabasco coast to the northern slope of the sierra of Chiapas. Today this terrain is pastureland when the season is dry enough and a swamp of flooded rivers and streams during the rainy season. One sees egrets and cranes hovering over the vast waters that are already crowded with ducks, grebes, and other waterfowl. The rains, heaviest in all of Mexico, have produced an exuberant tropical rain forest between the Palenque ruins and the adjacent mountains. At one time the valley was fertile land, rich for farming. Unnecessary burning and unchecked erosion, however, have greatly decreased the fertility of the soil and its productivity for farming. In the past the region had abundant natural resources, from the tropical forests to the grasslands and swamps. The Maya readily realized that this environment would be perfect for a ceremonial center and city: Palenque.

Just a short distance away flows the Usumacinta River, one of the great Maya "highways." The Maya, with no wheeled vehicles or draft animals, found waterways the easiest means of transportation. The Usumacinta was especially important because trade produce could move easily along the Bay of Campeche, then inland through the Usumacinta River system to the Petén. This important artery made possible communication between cities. Maya rulers, traveling in their great canoes, could participate in festivals and important ceremonial events in other cities, towns, and villages. Architects and artists could exchange views on the techniques and styles in vogue at each of the various centers. From the Usumacinta-Pasión river system communication routes extended overland through the Petén and north to the mountains of present-day Belize.

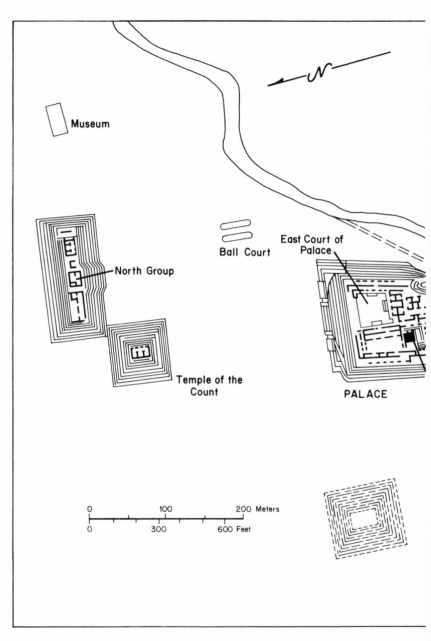

Palenque.

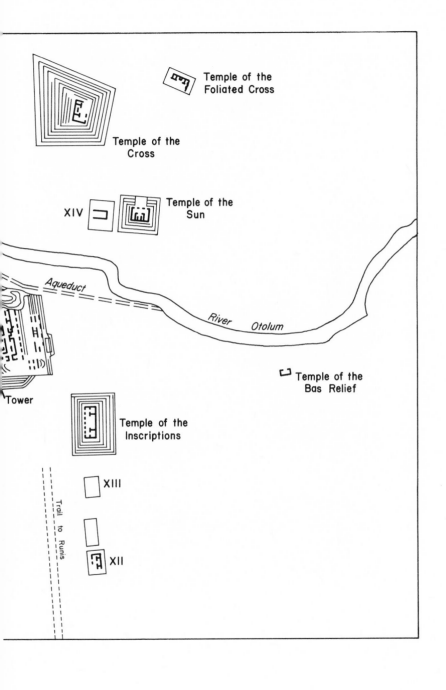

Temple of the
Foliated Cross

Temple of the
Cross

XIV

Temple of the
Sun

Aqueduct

River Otolum

Temple of the
Bas Relief

Tower

Temple of the
Inscriptions

XIII

Trail to Runis

XII

*An aerial view of Palenque. The largest building is the Palace.
Surrounding the Palenque ceremonial center today is a rain*

forest, which has overgrown hundreds of mounds, terraces, and platforms that were once parts of the center.

From there the Belize River flows to the Caribbean. Farther south, overland routes from the Petén linked up with the Motagua River and with other river systems used for transportation by the Maya. Because of this inland communication system, in addition to the coastal waterways, a degree of unity was established within the Maya civilization.

The elevated Palenque site commands a view of the great plains stretching to the distant horizon. Just five miles away is the little village of Santa Domingo Palenque, the closest town where the traveler can spend the night. The fern-covered mountains and wet forest behind the ruins act as a shimmering green screen for the great palace, the temples, and the residences that dot the surrounding hillsides. Natural hillocks were used as bases for some of the buildings, and where there were no such hillocks, the Maya built pyramids to elevate the buildings high above ground level. Some buildings were sheared against the mountainside, and artificial terraces and stairways were then constructed over this natural escarpment.

Judging from ceramic data, archaeologists think that Palenque was first occupied in the early or middle part of the Early Classic Period (A.D. 400–600), and possibly even in the Protoclassic Period. Early Classic pottery has been found under the Conde Pyramid (Temple of the Count) and in a burial underlying Temple XVIII, a small but important temple south of the Temple of the Foliated Cross. The major construction at Palenque took place during Late Classic times, specifically during the reign of the three kings Pacal the Great, Chan Bahlum II, and Kan Xul II. During the one-hundred-year period from A.D. 615 to 720, Palenque rose from a minor ceremonial center to a major western power.

Hillside towns and cities in which buildings were constructed at different levels on the sloping terrain were common along the lower Usumacinta. Wherever possible the buildings were oriented to the cardinal points, but most often the uneven terrain dictated the direction toward which the building faced. Palenque, Yaxchilán, and Piedras Negras were the largest and most imposing cities, with large ceremonial centers along the Usumacinta River, and each was distinctive in its plan, its architecture, and its sculpture.

As more research is carried out in the Maya area, we are gaining a better understanding of its political structure. For example, from recently deciphered hieroglyphic texts we now know that the Maya ruling families arranged marriages that allied major cities in a common bond. Also, large Maya cities were surrounded by smaller towns and villages that were often under the sovereignty of the city, and marriage alliances were sometimes arranged between ruling families of these areas.

Apparently each Maya city and its surrounding territory was autonomous. These loose-knit city-states were unified to the degree that religion, science, the arts, and other cultural, social, and economic endeavors were shared concerns.

The ruins of Palenque have been known since the eighteenth century. During the nineteenth century many noted archaeologists and a host of distinguished travelers visited the ruins. The list includes such names as John Lloyd Stephens and Alfred Maudslay, noted for their adventures throughout the Maya area; Frederick Waldeck, a classical artist who lived in one of the temples at Palenque for three years; Désiré Charnay; and Edward Thompson, who wrote articles on Palenque toward the end of the century. Shortly after that time Sylvanus G. Morley, Eduard G. Seler, and Franz Blom carried out archaeological reconnaissance at the site. Actual restoration was begun under the direction of Miguel Angel Fernández and was administered by the Mexican government. Later Alberto Ruz Lhuillier continued the restoration here, and it was he who made the remarkable discovery of the tomb in the Temple of the Inscriptions.

Palenque is one of the most beautifully conceived of all Maya cities. The architecture is inventive in design and well adapted to the humid climate. Originally the buildings were painted red and the stucco decoration green, yellow, and blue—a city in a blaze of colors. The brilliantly carved, delicate stucco reliefs on the piers, walls, and other parts of the buildings are of superb craftsmanship. The sculptures portray religious and secular ceremonies, and members of the ruling families. Some of the portraits were idealized, while others were highly realistic. Although some of the stucco-sculptured piers at Palenque depict considerable sacrifice and vio-

The west staircase leading to the Palace at Palenque. This palacelike structure underwent many additions and renovations over a period of several centuries. The four-storied tower dominates the area and is unique in Maya architecture. Late Classic.

lence, there must have been long periods of relative peace during which these people produced the beautifully sculptured figures on their buildings.

On approaching the archaeological zone, one sees many earthen mounds covered with dense undergrowth, indicating the work yet to be done by archaeologists. The full story of the magnificent ruins here has yet to be revealed. Even as we see it today, however, the site is awe-inspiring. Usually a light rain is blowing in over the mountains, creating a green mist that gives an effect similar to that of a Sung Dynasty painting. Against this soft yet lush green color stand the naked white buildings, denuded of their brilliant colors and stucco decorations by the centuries of almost constant tropical rains. Unfortunately, much of the sculpture at Palenque was done in stucco, one of the most perishable of all decorative materials when exposed to a rain-forest climate.

The Palace, a complicated network of buildings, vaulted galleries, patios, courtyards, porticoes, and subterranean chambers, was altered many times during its long occupancy. This imposing structure covers about an acre and is situated in a central area of the ceremonial city, so that the façades of most of the other buildings face toward it.

Although for the most part the Palace buildings are only a single story high, in the southwest corner is a tower four stories high, possibly built by Kan Xul, Chan Bahlum's brother. This tower may have been used as an astronomical observatory or as an observation post to announce the arrival of important guests from other cities. The tower is particularly important, however, in its relationship to the Temple of Inscriptions and may have been planned with that relationship in mind. At the winter solstice the sun sets in a direct line from the Palace tower to the center of the Temple of Inscriptions, where lies the tomb of Lord Pacal, Palenque's great ruler. Beneath the southern end of the Palace are subterranean chambers, indicating an earlier occupation here. The present Palace structures were no doubt built over these subterranean rooms at a later time, probably by Lord Pacal, and further additions to the Palace were made by his descendants.

The west side of the Palace is flanked by a palatial stairway leading to a porticoed chamber. The piers between the doorways of this vaulted chamber are of particular interest. Each of the five existing rectangular piers is decorated in stucco relief. A great deal of the stucco is missing or weatherworn, and the color has, of course, washed away except for scanty traces on some of the figures. The piers depict full figures of nobles dressed in ceremonial or courtly clothing. Most of the piers show a standing male figure attended by one or two persons in seated or kneeling positions. Palenque sculptors were masters in decorating buildings with stucco. They mixed fine-powdered lime with water into a paste and applied it to decorate walls and piers. The medium seems to have been ideal for the Maya temperament. On these decorations are some of the most exquisite lines, delicate contours, and sensitive expressions to be found in the pre-Columbian world. The elegance of the modeling contributes to a refinement in style that could have evolved only over a long period of time without major disruptions from external or internal forces. Although the west staircase to the Palace is the one used today, the main staircase is the one on the north side, and at one time it had a porticoed chamber with thirteen piers.

The Palace, like all the other buildings at Palenque, has a mansard-type roof that was completely stuccoed in bas-relief with delicately sculptured scenes representing rituals, ceremonies, deities, and other subjects in a highly conventionalized manner. Buildings were made taller by the addition of extremely high roof combs. As we see them today, the roof combs are perforated, but during Classic times they were covered with a carved-plaster embellishment and then painted. The roof combs are impressive against the green forest behind them. To see clearly the technique used to construct these combs, one can climb the stairway that circles the inside of the four-storied tower and then gaze down on the roof.

Several architectural features of the Palace are unusual. One of these is the great trilobate arch leading to the East Court. This same kind of arch was used in the construction of niches in the corbeled rooms and passageways inside the Palace, and it is found in other temple structures as well. The shape of the arches is

This stucco decoration on a pier of the Palace at Palenque depicts a narrative scene in which a standing dignitary is attended by two seated figures, one at each side. The person on the left is believed to be Lady Zac Kuk, a Palenque ruler. She was the mother of Pacal, who was entombed in the sarcophagus of the Temple of the Inscriptions. Astronomical glyphs frame the narrative scene.

The piers between the doorways of the porticoed chambers at Palenque are handsomely decorated in stucco. Persons adorned in ceremonial dress are important members of the ruling family. The figures stand on a base that represents plants and gods in the watery underworld.

reminiscent of those in the Islamic world. It is not unusual for similar art and architectural forms to develop independently in far-flung regions of the world; this trilobate arch is no exception.

In the East Court of the Palace are many panels and stairway facings carved in especially fine low relief. From the style of the sculpture and the alterations in the construction of the court, we can assume that many decorative and architectural changes were made over the centuries. In contrast to the usual formalistic style of Palenque figures are the nine larger-than-life figures on either side of the steps on the east stairway of the court. These figures, sculptured in an unparalleled naturalistic style, form a narrative

Details of a narrative scene on a pier of the Palace at Palenque. Although they are badly damaged by the weather, these stucco decorations are some of the most magnificent sculptures of their kind in the Maya world. The seated woman is wearing a belt, cape, and skirt of jade beads. Late Classic.

The East Court of the Palace at Palenque. Where a section of the mansard roof has fallen, it is possible to see the corbeled trilobate openings between the Palace walls. On both

sides of the stairway to the court are sculptured panels depicting narrative scenes. These panels may have been a later addition to the court. Late Classic.

On the right side of the stairs to the East Court of the Palace at Palenque are five human figures sculptured in low relief. An exception to the usual formal Classic Maya style encountered at Palenque, this narrative scene is sculptured in a realistic provincial style.

scene. The two figures closest to the stairs have their heads turned up as though paying respect to someone at the top. Six of the other figures may be priests or members of the ruling family who have been involved in handing down some kind of judgment. The ninth figure, on the extreme right, may represent the person receiving the judgment, for he is the only one in the nude; he may have come to this disgrace by departing from the mores of the society.

Detail of the figure at the left in the preceding photograph. It shows the skillful rendering by the sculptor of a member of Maya society.

The expression on his face is one of great anxiety. These sculptures obviously were not designed for this court but were moved here from some older structure.

On the opposite side of this court are two more oversize figures on the balustrade of the stairs. They are similar to the figures carved in stone on the balustrade of the top platform of the Temple of the Inscriptions, and the two carvings may date from the same period. The hieroglyphs on the west stairway of the East Court (House C) of the Palace record the birth of Pacal in A.D. 603, which is probably the dedicatory date of the building.

Close examination of the east and west courts of the Palace indicates that these carved panels on the lower portion of the platforms surrounding the courts were a later addition, made during

141

one of the many renovations. They may have been added to reinforce the substructure of the courts as well as to enhance their beauty.

Palenque is noted for a series of finely carved limestone panels and tablets. One of these is on a wall of a porticoed chamber (Building E) on the south side of the Palace. This oval plaque, carved in relief, commemorates the accession of Pacal, who ruled Palenque from A.D. 615 to 683. The woman on the left is his mother, the queen Zac-Kuk, who is shown transferring the rule to her son. The most important tablet found in Palenque was unearthed in the north end of the Palace by Alberto Ruz Lhuillier (see below). It dates from the end of the seventh century and is called the Tablet of the Palace. It is now in the Palenque Museum.

Throughout the Palace are indications of patterned designs painted on the plaster on both the external and the internal walls. A steam bath, urinals fed by water ducts from running streams under the floor of the Palace, altars, throne benches, air vents, and other utilitarian innovations can be seen in various parts of the structures. The very high vaulted ceilings here as well as in other buildings in this archaeological zone were designed to keep the rooms cool, another important architectural innovation of the Maya at Palenque. The use of double-vaulted ceilings, porticoes, and doorways made the rooms light and airy, especially in comparison with the dark, small chambers in the temple buildings at Tikal, in the Petén. It would seem that this palace was much more functional than those at other Maya cities. The dozens of rooms for the housing of such persons as the rulers, chiefs, priests, and lesser nobles indicate a large populace at the ceremonial center. The large rooms with spacious open courts at the northern and eastern ends of the Palace were most likely those reserved for ruling families. Smaller apartments and rooms at the southern end of the Palace may have been used by visiting guests and persons of noble status. Other rooms may have been servants' quarters or utility rooms.

The Temple of the Inscriptions, one of the great monumental structures at Palenque, was built as a mortuary shrine after the death of Lord Pacal. Its fame is due to the tireless energy of the remarkable archaeologist Alberto Ruz Lhuillier (1970). It was he

The Temple of the Inscriptions, at Palenque, famed for its burial chamber. It rises on a terraced platform backed against a steep hillside. It was here that Alberto Ruz Lhuillier discovered the stairway leading to the tomb of Lord Pacal, buried here in an elaborate chamber within a stone sarcophagus in A.D. 683.

who discovered the secret passage in 1948 and during the following four seasons excavated the stairway that leads to the magnificent royal tomb of Palenque's greatest ruler, Lord Pacal.

Eight stepped terraces form the base of the pyramid that is crowned by the Temple of the Inscriptions. The terraces are edged with binding moldings that create pleasant horizontal frames for

143

each terrace. A single narrow stairway without a balustrade leads to the top of the pyramid. Part of the back of the pyramid is built into the side of a steep limestone hill. Behind the temple a tropical forest frames the structure, giving it dimension. The mansardlike roof, once covered with stucco, had an ornate roof comb, but little of it is left today. This building is the highest at Palenque, rising seventy-five feet above the plaza. The roof comb adds approximately forty feet to the height of the structure. The five doorways to the temple are separated by four piers decorated in stucco in the same style as that on the Palace. All four piers depict a similar theme and may form a narrative sequence. An important person, perhaps a Palenque lord, holds in his arms a child, who is probably the young prince Chan-Bahlum. The decoration on one of these piers depicts a person of noble class wearing a jaguar-skin skirt and an apron of jade beads. The apron is similar to the one carved on Stela H at Copán. Both long and short skirts are depicted in Maya paintings and on their sculptures and reliefs. These garments do not, however, denote the sex of the person, and one needs other physical or hieroglyphic information to identify a figure.

Through the piers of the Temple of the Inscriptions one enters a large vaulted chamber with three panels containing one of the longest of Maya hieroglyphic inscriptions. The panels were dedicated in A.D. 692. Glyphs on the panels cover a chronology of about two hundred years and record data of historical significance regarding dynastic rule, such as the names of rulers and their accession dates. Important ending ceremonies and historical events in the life of Lord Pacal are recorded here as well.

One of the keys to finding the secret stairway leading to the tomb was the discovery of circular holes, plugged with stone inserts, in a slab of the floor. These holes were used to lower the large stone slab into place when the Maya closed the tomb. The descent down the tunnellike stairway can be accomplished with the aid of a flashlight; there is electricity at Palenque, but power failure has been known to occur. Since the famed tomb is five feet below the level of the plaza, one must descend the dark, damp, slippery stairway to a level eighty feet below the temple floor. To peer into the tomb and see the sarcophagus would be a thrilling moment

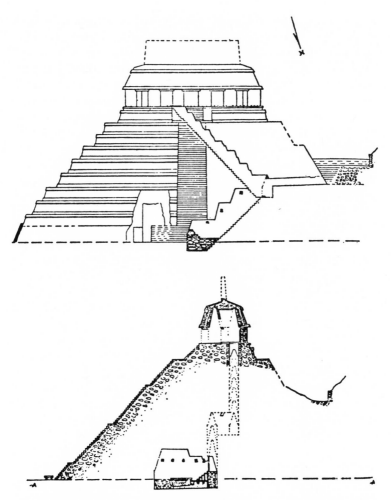

The Temple of the Inscriptions, Palenque. Elevation and section show-
ing the interior staircase leading from the rear room of the temple to
the burial crypt. An air duct led from the stairway landing to the ex-
terior of the pyramid. After A. Ruz, from Thompson, The Rise and Fall
of Maya Civilization.

in anyone's life. Even though the contents of the tomb have been moved to the Museum of Anthropology in Mexico City, the sarcophagus, with its beautiful bas-relief carving, is still here. The sides depict in stucco Pacal's ruling ancestors. The sarcophagus lid, weighing five tons, has a sculptured relief on the top depicting the story of death and rebirth. The exquisitely carved figure on the lid is believed to represent Lord Pacal descending into the underworld. The border of the relief is carved with celestial glyphs. The walls of the crypt are decorated with nine stucco figures which Linda Schele and others believe represent historical persons rather than mythological ones. Other archaeologists believe that the figures depict the nine lords of the underworld.

Inside the sarcophagus were the remains of the ruler and his ceremonial attire. He was covered with jade ornaments: earplugs, pendants, beads, rings for each finger of both hands, and a mask consisting of two hundred pieces of brilliant green jade. Also in the tomb were a smaller jade mask representing an old man, two beautiful jade figurines, and two life-size stucco heads. The two heads had been broken at the neck, indicating that they were removed from some other part of the ceremonial center and placed here when the crypt was closed. The stylized faces of both heads suggest the sensitivity of the carving. Pieces of jade were placed in the mouth of the dead ruler and in each hand, a burial custom similar to that of the ancient Chinese. The pottery pieces also found in the tomb probably contained food and drink as offerings to the gods. Before the tomb was closed, the whole chamber was sprinkled with powdered red cinnabar, widely used in burials throughout Mesoamerica. The red color symbolizes the east, the rising sun, and resurrection.

Outside the tomb wall were found the skeletons of several youths who may have been left to guard the tomb. When the Maya had finished the burial, they used rubble to fill the stairway that leads to the temple above. In planning the stairway, the architects designed an air duct to run from the tomb up the side of the stairs to the temple floor. This duct can be seen today. The air passage may have been intended to serve as a means of communication from the crypt to the celestial world of the Maya deities.

Stela B at Copán is one of the many handsomely carved monuments that have made this ceremonial center famous. The stela depicts a Maya ruler and bears the dedication date A.D. 731.

One of the most interesting of the sculptured monuments in the Great Plaza at Copán is a spherical "altar" encircled by a design of entwined rope. The significance of this so-called altar is unknown.

In the East Court at Copán is a monumental sculpture believed to be dedicated to the planet Venus. In the center is a head that represents the sun deity Kinich Ahau. Late Classic.

This fine, large bead of white and green marbleized jade was found in the burial of an elite Maya in the ceremonial site Toniná. It bears the date A.D. *731. Courtesy American Museum of Natural History.*

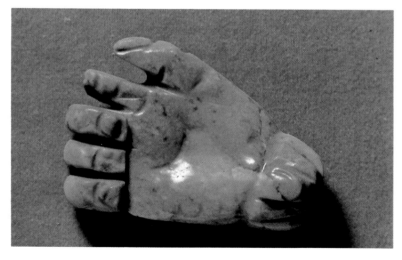

A jade talisman shaped like a hand was one of the burial pieces found with the Toniná jades. Courtesy American Museum of Natural History.

The Great Plaza and North Acropolis of Tikal as seen from the air. The North Acropolis is Early Classic superimposed with many Late Classic buildings. Courtesy Mrs. Paul Williams.

Temple III emerges above the treetops at Tikal. This temple, 180 feet high, may be the mortuary shrine of the Late Classic ruler Chitam.

Stucco portraits of the Maya are highly stylized. This particular portrait (left) is of a young Maya elite, sensitively carved and then painted. Tabasco Museum. Late Classic.

Portrait (right) of a Maya dignitary dressed in ceremonial clothing. This detail is part of a larger plaque in the Tabasco Museum in Villahermosa.

In the East Court of the Palace at Palenque a story is narrated in sculpture. This (left) is one of the nine figures assembled on the sides of the court stairway.

In the village of Sayaxché, Guatemala, is a remarkable stela from La Amelia depicting a Maya personage dressed in ceremonial regalia (right). Late Classic.

Of all the ceremonial buildings at Palenque, the Temple of the Inscriptions is the most famous because of the funeral chamber of Lord Pacal found under the pyramid. It contained a rich treasure of jades. Lord Pacal, Palenque's greatest ruler, died in A.D. 683.

In the lush rain forest along the Usumacinta River is the Maya ceremonial center Yaxchilán. Structure 41 is one of the many hundreds of buildings here that have not been restored. Late Classic.

Much of the ceremonial center at Yaxchilán is buried under the jungle floor. Only the roof comb of Structure 5, shown here, is above ground; the rest of the building is intact below the surface. Late Classic.

The Palace of the Masks at Kabáh is one of the very impressive palacelike buildings in the Puuc Hills of Yucatán. Late Classic.

Part of the Palace at Sayil in the Puuc Hills. The porticoed chambers on the second floor at one time opened onto patios. Limestone was the building material of most of the structures in the Northern Lowlands.

Entrance to an important courtyard at Labná is through the portal arch, the most beautiful arch constructed by the Maya.

The Palace at Labná. The Palace is one of the largest buildings of its kind in the Puuc Hills. Most of it has not been restored. Late Classic.

The west side of the House of the Magician in the afternoon sun, Uxmal. Late Classic.

Detail showing a warrior on the West Structure of the Nunnery Quadrangle at Uxmal.

*On the edge of a cliff, overlooking the Caribbean Sea, stands Tulúm.
Late Postclassic.*

The Observatory at Chichén Itzá. Earlier superimpositions here are Maya and date from Classic times. Later superimpositions show Mexicanized Maya influence.

East Annex of the Nunnery at Chichén Itzá. An elaborate façade was created with hundreds of mosaic stones. The Maya rain-god mask is the leitmotiv. Late Classic.

The Castillo at Chichén Itzá in the setting sun. Postclassic. Courtesy Alice Brody.

The four small temples in this area of Palenque are noted for the beautifully carved panels in the inner sanctuaries. Hieroglyphs on the back panel of this structure, the Temple of the Sun, give the date corresponding to A.D. 642.

Rising from artificial platforms that were once plastered and painted are the Temple of the Cross, the Temple of the Foli-

ated Cross, and the Temple of the Sun. All these structures at Palenque were built during Late Classic times.

At Tres Zapotes and Monte Albán stone-and-clay tubes have been found in burials more than a thousand years older than this tomb.

The tomb under the Temple of the Inscriptions is not the only one at Palenque; excavations have revealed over a thousand burials in this ceremonial area. Lord Pacal's tomb, however, contained by far the most outstanding treasure found at the site and in style is unique in the Americas.

Looking eastward from the Palace, one can see four small temples similar to one another in design, all of them on artificial terraces with pyramidal bases. The most impressive of these pyramids is the Temple of the Sun because of its great roof comb, which is partly intact. Depicted here is a seated ruler holding a ceremonial bar and surrounded by gods. The piers and the mansard-like roof also contained stucco sculptures, little of which remains today. The other three pyramids, the Temple of the Cross, the Temple of the Foliated Cross, and Temple XIV, are noted for their superb relief sculptures carved on limestone tablets. The temples face a central plaza which may have been important for festivities in this part of the ceremonial center. All four buildings were highly ornamented in stucco, including the high roof combs and the walls to the façades; stucco friezes adorned the roofs.

Of greatest importance in each of these temples are the superb limestone panels carved in low relief and mounted on the wall at the rear of the inner-vaulted sanctuary. According to Mathews and Schele, after Lord Pacal's death Lord Chan Bahlum, his son, ascended to the throne. The Temple of the Sun, the Temple of the Cross, and the Temple of the Foliated Cross are believed to have been built in honor of his ascendancy, and the tablets in these sanctuaries may represent the conveying of the rule from father to son. The panel in the Temple of the Cross was removed to the National Museum of Anthropology and History in Mexico City.

One of our earliest portrayals of a person smoking a cigar is carved on a panel at the right of the central doorway in the Temple of the Cross. Sir J. Eric S. Thompson believed that sapodilla or allspice leaves were used to wrap the tobacco. Tobacco was also powdered and mixed with lime in much the same way that a mixture of pepper vines and lime is used by people of the South

150

Seas. Lime activates the chemicals in the tobacco or pepper vines and produces a stimulant. Coca leaves are used in much the same way today by the people of Peru and Bolivia.

The panel on the left side of the doorway of the Temple of the Cross has a magnificent carving of Lord Chan-Bahlum. This imposing figure wears some of the most resplendent ceremonial dress to be seen in the Maya world. Adjacent to the Temple of the Sun is the recently excavated and partly restored Structure XIV. This temple is similar in design to the other three here but is believed to be of later date. The sculpture depicts a woman presenting a manikin god (God K) to the ruler, probably Chan Bahlum.

Hieroglyphs are an integral part of the design of the panels found in both the temples and the Palace. The dates on the temple panels suggest a span from A.D. 642 to 692. The Palace panels have later dates, 720 and 783. The Temple of the Sun has had the most restoration and is in fair condition. Neither of the pyramids of the Temple of the Cross or the Temple of the Foliated Cross has been restored, however, and the front half of the Temple of the Foliated Cross long ago collapsed and tumbled down the embankment. Nevertheless, from the platform of this temple a superb view of the whole ceremonial center and the surrounding countryside is possible on a clear day.

During the rainy season hundreds of little streams swell into rivers and pour down from the limestone cliffs behind the ceremonial center into the Otolum River. Maya engineers designed a system of bridges over this river to provide access to the temples on the other side. In addition to the bridges they built a vaulted stone aqueduct nine feet high to direct the stream under the plaza floor. During late spring and summer when the rains are not heavy, the Otolum River dwindles to a little stream. Not too many years ago, when travelers slept in hammocks in the village and there were no washing facilities, this stream was handy for a quick bath —quite refreshing after a hot day in the sun.

Between the Palace and what is called the North Group is a small, unrestored ball court that is believed to be Early Classic. The North Group consists of five buildings on platforms at different levels, flanked by stairs. Varying greatly in size and prob-

Temple III, a small oratorylike structure, in the North Group at Palenque. During the Classic Period this structure was plastered and painted.

ably in function, the buildings may have been used for religious or other ceremonial events during the Late Classic Period.

West of the North Group is the Temple of the Count, so called because Frederick Waldeck may have used the building as a residence or studio. During his three years here in the early nineteenth century he made a series of drawings of the Palenque reliefs. Waldeck was convinced of the Egyptian origin of the Maya

152

civilization, and his fanciful drawings were executed in the "Egyptian style." They were in no way related to the original Maya carvings, however. The Temple of the Count has been more nearly completely restored than have other buildings in the North Group. The structure is believed to be the oldest building in this area.

Just east of the North Group is a small museum housing some of the treasures found at Palenque. Here it is possible to examine carefully the Tablet of the Palace, the large panel of glyphs found in the Palace. The scene at the top of the tablet shows Lord Kan Xul, ruler of Palenque in the late seventh century, in the center. He is flanked by Lord Pacal, his father, on the left and by Lady Ahpo-Hel, his mother, on the right. As on other Palenque tablets, the left figure presents the ruler's jade-encrusted headdress, and the right figure offers a platter containing a shield. All three figures are seated on stacked mats that signify thrones.

The left vertical panel of the Tablet of the Palace consists of rare full-figure glyphs that express periods of time. The top glyph, the Initial Series glyph, depicts the patron god of the month, Mac. The glyph blocks below it depict on the left a god of a number. The grotesque figure on the left represents the period of time.

The museum also has a collection of beautiful stuccos, jade pieces, funerary urns, pottery, and other objects excavated at Palenque. Just outside the museum is Palenque's only stela. The center of the stone shaft projects from each side; it is a poor imitation of Copán's stelae in the round.

Palenque was not a city of tall pyramids or great stelae, nor was it a city that produced much pottery. Ceramic evidence indicates that its history began in Preclassic times and its flowering took place during the Late Classic Period (A.D. 600-900). The carved-stucco decorations are highly stylized in a manner unique to Palenque. The refinement and subtlety of these low-relief sculptures make them, aside from their historical significance, the finest artistic expressions from the ancient world that survive today. The linear style is in great contrast to the robust, rococo style of the artists of Copán. Each city was a part of the great Maya tradition: Copán was the foremost center in the southern limits of the Maya world, and Palenque in the westernmost sector. In the ar-

153

chitecture of both geographical extremities the horizontal line is dominant. This is emphasized by binding moldings that encircle terraces, cornices, doorways, and platforms. The moldings create shadows that stress the horizontal line and thus act as a unifying force for the entire architectural complex. There is a close tectonic relationship with the terrain in the placement of the buildings at different levels. The Maya city planners always seemed to be conscious of the environment and the terrain on which they were to build. At Palenque in particular a harmony prevails between the natural forces and the efforts of man.

Yaxchilán

In the last few years considerable work has been done at Yaxchilán. The lower bench has been cleared, making it easier to find buildings and sculptures there. Paths have been cleared to the most important structures on the steep hillsides. The especially fine Structure 33 is reached by a grand staircase that starts its ascent from the lower bench adjacent to the Usumacinta River. Most of the ruins, however, still lie largely buried under earthen mounds that have been cleared of trees and scrub. Many buildings project above the mounds covering the substructures. Over the doorways of these temples and palacelike buildings are the handsomely carved lintels that have made Yaxchilán one of the most outstanding of Maya ceremonial centers in terms of fine stone carving.

Yaxchilán is in the state of Chiapas, on the southwest bank of the Usumacinta River, which separated Guatemala from Mexico. The river flows through the Usumacinta Valley, creating on either side shallow benches of flatland suitable for agriculture. Steep embankments with deep ravines lead away from the river basin. This tropical forest receives one of the heaviest rainfalls in Mexico.

The name Yaxchilán is Maya for Green Stones; the color is caused by algae in an adjoining river, the Arroyo Yaxchilán. Many important scholars visited the ruins at the end of the nineteenth century, including Teobert Maler, Alfred P. Maudslay, and Désiré Charnay. At the beginning of the twentieth century Alfred M.

Yaxchilán and Piedras Negras were two major Maya cities along the Usumacinta River, shown here. This waterway was extremely important to the Maya as a route for trade goods from the Gulf of Mexico to the Petén and the Guatemala Highlands.

Tozzer, Sylvanus G. Morley, Herbert J. Spinden, and others visited here. One of the most valuable accounts of Yaxchilán is given in Morley's *Inscriptions of Petén.*

The ceremonial center of Yaxchilán consists of a number of groupings of buildings, courtyards, and plazas studded with stelae and altars. The major groupings extend along the bench of the river basin for a thousand yards. The extremely steep hills and deep

155

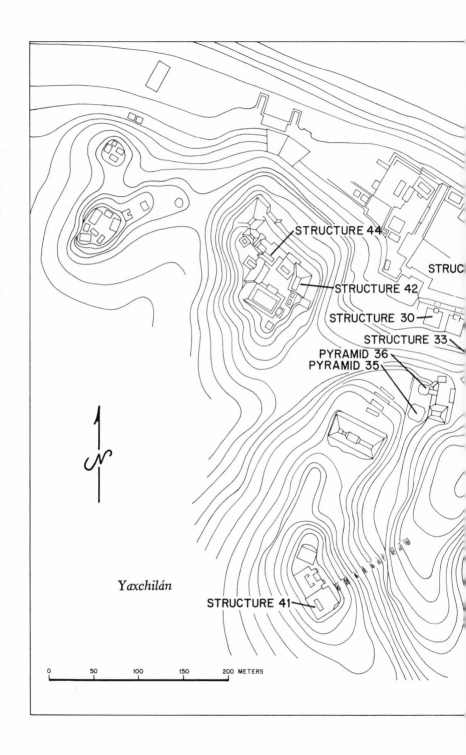

STRUCTURE 44

STRUC

STRUCTURE 42

STRUCTURE 30

STRUCTURE 33

PYRAMID 36
PYRAMID 35

Yaxchilán

STRUCTURE 41

0   50   100   150   200 METERS

ravines farther back from the river separate other groupings. On the very tops of these hills, some 300 to 360 feet high, are many other structures. These hillsides were terraced with cut stone, now buried under the forest floor. Buildings erected on these artificial plateaus are not oriented to the cardinal points but instead follow the contours of the ravines. Most of these structures face the Main Plaza along the river basin.

The intensity of the heat and humidity along the Usumacinta River was a factor in the placement and design of many of the buildings. The structures high on the hilltops were designed as residences and temples for the rulers and religious leaders of the city-state. Here there was a cooler and more frequent breeze, sunlight more quickly dried the plazas and courtyards between the frequent rains, and the elite could escape the humidity created by the river. That part of the city along the benches of the river was accessible to the laboring class, craftsmen, and merchants. Canoes, other kinds of boats, and rafts plied the river, bringing in goods for the capital city and transporting people from other territories who had business at the ceremonial center.

The buildings were made of cut limestone with high, narrow, vaulted chambers, and many had porticoes. These factors were all-important to Yaxchilán architects in planning for rooms to be cool and dry. A similar architectural style is found at Palenque and Piedras Negras. Constant plastering kept moisture from seeping into the limestone and protected it from plant growth. Painting the buildings and plazas softened the light and enhanced the beauty of the structures for all to enjoy, to admire, and to praise. To decorate the high roof combs, porticoes, and other exterior architectural elements, sculptors created imagery in stucco and stone. Inscriptions were incised on stelae, altars, lintels, and stairways.

Much of the subject matter for relief carving at Yaxchilán concerns warfare, prisoners and their captors, ceremonial life, scenes of penitential bloodletting, and visionary scenes. The concern with warfare, a dominant theme in stone reliefs, indicates political unrest in this westernmost sector of the Maya territory. In a stone relief on Lintel 26 an unusually long quilted bib is shown being worn around a warrior's neck. It was evidently a kind of

Among the many fragments of stone sculpture at Yaxchilán is this one, depicting a person either giving or receiving a string of beads to or from the dignitary standing above. This monument may originally have been part of a stela or panel on a wall of a residential structure.

armor used for combat and was unique to this area. A similar bib is noted in Jaina figurines, but to date they have not been found in other areas occupied by the Maya.

The Yaxchilán sculptors enjoyed depicting group scenes on their monuments, a theme also popular at Piedras Negras. The most famous example of the Piedras Negras narrative scenes is Stela 12, in which eight prisoners are shown in anguish at the feet of an autocratic ruler. Yaxchilán had the advantage of proximity to the great cities of Palenque and Piedras Negras. The style of some monuments and use of certain glyphs, however, reflected the influence of such distant Maya centers as those in the Puuc Hills of Yucatán. Yaxchilán composition and carving lacked the grace, rhythm, and proportion of the sculptures at Piedras Negras. Yet at the height of Yaxchilán's development there is a vigor of design and a refinement in stone carving. The aesthetic quality of stone carving at Yaxchilán was maintained at a high level until the mid-eighth century. After that the quality declined.

The sculptured reliefs of Yaxchilán give important information about the rulers and their families, some of whom have been identified. Tatiana Proskouriakoff identified several of the dynastic rulers at both Yaxchilán and Piedras Negras and has deciphered other pertinent glyphic data as well. It is interesting to note that at Yaxchilán, according to Tatiana Proskouriakoff, women played a very important social role and are depicted on many of the relief sculptures.

The Main Plaza at Yaxchilán extends approximately three hundred yards along the Usumacinta River. Around this plaza are a great number of structures that may have served as residences, storage areas for ceremonial equipment, or religious buildings. Platforms surrounding the plaza could have served as market areas and places for special ceremonies. The main plazas of most ceremonial centers had ball courts. Two ball courts at Yaxchilán are in the area of the Main Plaza; the one on the west side of the plaza contains circular playing markers, three in the alley of the court and two on the benches of the court.

On a steep hilltop approximately two hundred feet above the Main Plaza stands Structure 33, one of the most important build-

Structure 33, one of the major temple buildings at Yaxchilán. Above the doorways are niches to hold sculptures. At one time the temple had a high roof comb. Much of this structure has been destroyed by encroaching tree roots. The area has had no major excavation or restoration.

ings at Yaxchilán. Terraces extend from the Main Plaza to this temple or palace structure, creating an impressive cascade of platforms. When one looks upward, this building assumes monumental proportions and acts as a focal point for the ceremonial center. When the great Maya lords and their retinues descended these stairs, they must have provided a dramatic spectacle for the populace watching from the plaza below.

161

Hieroglyphs sculptured in low relief can be seen in many parts of Yaxchilán. This panel of glyphs is on one of the steps at the entrance to Structure 44.

Structure 33 has three doorways leading into a single long chamber, a kind of room that is common in Maya buildings. The structure has an extremely beautiful roof comb that runs the whole length of the building. The roof comb is perforated in an open geometric design, and in its center is a large image of a seated deity. The mansardlike roof was also covered with stucco figures, little of which remains today.

Continuing up the steep hillside from Structure 33 are platforms, terraces, and stairways that lead to a group of three buildings at the city's highest point, the South Acropolis, 360 feet above the Usumacinta River. On this pinnacle Structure 41 dominates the hilltop. There are two other buildings here with dimensions and floor plans similar to those of Structure 41. Structure 41 shows some indication that there was a frieze of plaster hieroglyphs just below the cornice. A great stairway descends from the façade of this building to a platform three hundred feet below the South Acropolis. The stairway is broken by ten sections in which pylons are incorporated into the architectural design. This esplanade of stairs, platforms, and terracing, decorated with stelae, altars, and other sculptures, must have been an extremely impressive sight.

Directly northwest of the South Acropolis is the West Acropolis, on a hilltop that rises 230 feet above the Usumacinta. This acropolis consists of a number of mounds and several large structures still hidden in the tropical forest. The best preserved of these is Structure 44. On this building one can see superb carved lintels on three doorways, and the doorsteps are carved in finely executed hieroglyphs. The whole platform was terraced down to the river basin below. Stairways were flanked by pylons, as were the great stairways to Structures 33 and 41. In front of Structure 44 were five stelae. Yaxchilán has many dedicatory stelae and altars; there are forty-four such carved monuments and many more left uncarved. Still others may be uncovered during future excavations. Of the many buildings here seventeen have a combined total of fifty-three carved lintels.

Yaxchilán, with its impressive ceremonial center, was one of the major cities of the Maya along the Usumacinta River. The extent of its territory is unknown, but the strong influence of Yaxchilán on Bonampak sculpture suggests that Yaxchilán may also have controlled Bonampak and adjacent towns and villages, at least for some time. In any event, today the ruins lie blanketed with moss and lichen, and most of the city is buried far below the surface of the forest floor. Over the years great numbers of sculptures have been removed from Yaxchilán by museums and collectors. Vandals and looters have recently done great damage to this and many other Maya sites. It can only be hoped that Mexico will someday uncover more of this ceremonial center and provide the caretakers necessary to ensure that the world can see another of the spectacular cities of the Maya.

Bonampak

It seems an irony that the most precious of all pre-Columbian paintings in Mesoamerica lie deep in a tropical rain forest in a remote area of Chiapas and are rarely seen by man. The jungle here is covered with a canopy of branches of such trees as chicle and mahogany. This verdant blanket is broken by the palo blanco tree, which in the springtime forms an umbrella of yellow flowers that shower the jungle trails. This little-known wilderness area, sparsely settled by a few Lacondon, contains groups of archaeological sites in the surrounding countryside no farther than thirty miles away, including Ojos de Agua, Lacanhá, Oxlahuntún, Miguel Angel Fernández, and Tzendales.

Although John Bourne and H. Carl Fry explored Bonampak in February, 1946, they did not see the temple known as Structure 1 with its famous murals. It was Giles G. Healey who discovered the temple just four months later, in May, 1946, and informed the outside world of his great discovery.

On approaching the ceremonial center, one first encounters a small plaza surrounded by low-lying mounds. From here most of the structures at Bonampak can be seen. They are arranged on platforms on a natural hillside terraced with limestone. The buildings at Bonampak are simple in design and, except for Structure 1, have only a single room. There are similarities in the architectural

The plaza area at Bonampak, looking toward the great stairway. The ruins have been only partly excavated, and many mounds in the forest remain untouched. The distant hill is part of the elaborate platforms that are now covered with soil and vegetation. Structures 1 and 2 are in the right and left foreground.

design of the structures and in the carvings of stone lintels to those of Yaxchilán. Both Morley and Ruppert compared architectural details at Bonampak to those at Piedras Negras. It is now known through the research of Peter Mathews that Bonampak and Yaxchilán had a very close relationship, beginning in Early Classic times. They may have been allies in battles with nearby villages.

165

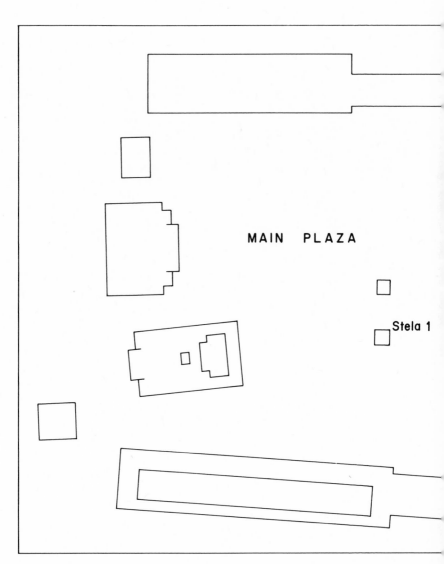

MAIN PLAZA

Stela 1

Bonampak. After Ruppert and Stromsvik.

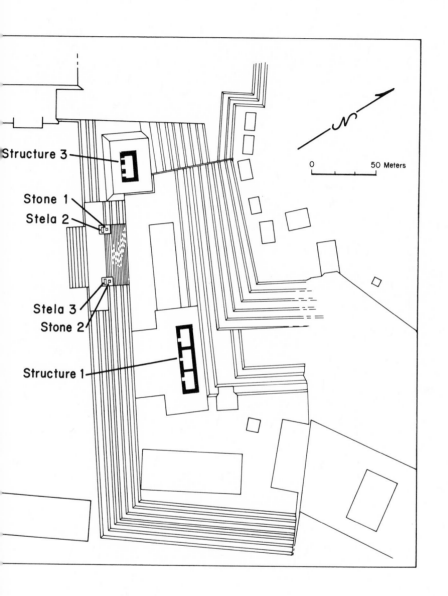

Structure 3

Stone 1

Stela 2

Stela 3

Stone 2

Structure 1

0   50 Meters

Detail of Stela 1, at Bonampak, showing how the sculptor executed a difficult hand gesture. The long, curved nose, the flattened forehead, the receding chin, and downturned lip line are typical of the Late Classic style. It is not unusual to find a fish form ornamenting the nose or forming part of the headdress, in which the fish is nibbling on a lotus.

We can assume that they had economic ties as well. Areas farther down the Usumacinta would have come under the control of Piedras Negras.

The largest of the stelae at Bonampak is Stela 1, recently reassembled and replaced in its original position in the Main Plaza. The elaborately costumed personage on the front of the stela is carved in the usual ornate style, but on this particular stela the ideals of Maya beauty have been largely ignored. Still, the beautiful detail of the tracery on the mask form on which the figure is standing is especially fine.

Stela 2 (A.D. 783), at Bonampak, portrays the ruler Chaan-Muan. The woman standing behind him, Lady Yax Rabbit, is probably his wife. His mother stands in front of him holding the sacrificial perforator.

A detail of the head of Stela 2 beautifully displays the style of the very high headdress worn during Late Classic times. The jade earrings, beads, and mantle are typical ornaments worn by the Maya in cities and towns along the Usumacinta River.

Structure 1 houses the famed Bonampak murals. The building is covered with modern superstructure to protect it from the tropical rains. Bonampak is a Late Classic site.

Stelae 2 and 3 are on the great stairway adjoining the Plaza and are carved in the same style as that of the lintels in Structure 1. Stela 2 is a particularly fine carving portraying the ruler Chan Muan. He is attended by two women, Lady Yax Rabbit, who may be his wife, and, in front of him, his mother. Both are dressed in the splendid ceremonial costumes befitting important ladies attending a mighty lord. His headdress is impressive in its height and delicate in the assemblage of its components. The recurrent Maya image of a fish nibbling on a water lily is found on the front of the headdress of the lady on his right.

The great stairway ascends to the first platform, on which Structures 1 and 3 stand. It is important to enter Structure 3, for

171

this building contains a large stucco head that must have once decorated the façade of some structure at Bonampak. The head lies on the floor of the temple, no doubt placed there to prevent further damage by the elements or by vandals. Structure 1 is now protected from drenching rains by a canopy of corrugated metal, and it is in this building that the famed Bonampak murals can be seen. Not far from Bonampak are two additional sites, Maudslay and Bee Ruin, that reportedly once had murals on their walls. Fortunately, the murals at Bonampak have been partly preserved by a coating of calcium bicarbonate produced by moisture reacting chemically with the limestone. These murals are now over a thousand years old. On parts of them the color of the paint is still as brilliant as though freshly applied, although in recent years there has been progressive deterioration.

Structure 1 has three doorways, each with carved stone lintels. The carvings depict a warrior and his captive, and glyphs are arranged as an integral part of the lintel design. These lintels are similar to those in Structure 44 at Yaxchilán. Above the doorway is a medial molding running the length of the façade. Over this molding are three niches that at one time contained seated stucco figures. The upper façade of the building was decorated in stucco relief, little of which remains today.

All three rooms of Structure 1 are identical in size, and all of them are encircled by low benches that would make comfortable seating or convenient shelves for ceremonial paraphernalia. The walls of all three rooms are covered with painted murals. The composition of the different structural shapes within the room, the masterly outline drawings of the figures, and the beautiful rendering of the paintings display the high quality of workmanship and artistry attained by the Maya.

Sir J. Eric S. Thompson interpreted in an interesting way the story depicted on the murals. The narrative begins in Room 1 with a scene of important personages preparing for a raid on some nearby village. The scene is a realistic one clearly depicting the action, the manners, the social classes, the dress, and the ceremonial regalia of the eighth-century Maya. Wars were an activity of the elite class, commanding great prestige for its members. The lower section of the mural represents musicians and masked participants in a processional. In Room 2 the story is continued; we see a dramatic scene of the actual raid, showing warriors and their enemies engaged in battle. A second scene in the same room could be called the "judgment scene," and it is here that we see the prisoners being arraigned before the great lords of Bonampak. The mural in Room 3 portrays the sacrifice of one of the prisoners and the pleading of the others for mercy. The celebration and dance that follow, in which the lords, nobles, and dancers are portrayed in their richest ceremonial garments, dramatically ends the story.

There are many other scenes depicted on the murals in this building, showing the various activities of the chief, the two women with him, a child, the nobles, the attendants, and the other persons involved in the raid and the ceremony. Each section of the mural is alive with detail. The expressive line used to render the human figure, the facial features revealing great emotion, and the wealth of the ceremonial attire have no equal in any other culture in the Americas. The blue and orange-yellow colors used in Room 1 are brilliant beyond belief. The painting is in true fresco, but it appears that some color was applied after the plaster was dry. The colors used for the mural were analyzed and were found to be of mineral composition, except for black, a wood ash.

The Bonampak murals must have been one of hundreds of groups of murals painted by the Maya. Time and the elements have eroded and destroyed most of them. The murals surviving at Bonampak rank with the great artistic masterpieces of all time.

6   The Pasión River: Seibal

The rain forest at Seibal has a lush green canopy sprinkled with the orange patches of the beautiful amapola tree. In full bloom this tree blazes like a fire against the blue tropical sky. The great ceiba trees along the Pasión River have given Seibal its name— Spanish for Place of the Ceiba Tree. Approximately ten miles up the river are two palm-thatched huts, the headquarters used from 1964 to 1968 by archaeologists Gordon R. Willey and A. Ledyard Smith, of Harvard University. The university decided to excavate at Seibal after work had been completed at Altar de Sacrificios, seventy-five miles down the Pasión River. Earlier research here was carried out by Teobert Maler in 1895 and 1905, and Sylvanus G. Morley undertook a more thorough investigation in 1914.

During Classic times there were many important cities along the Pasión and Usumacinta rivers. Piedras Negras and Yaxchilán are two of the larger cities farther down the river. In the center of each city was the ceremonial area for religious, social, and political activities. It is this part of each city that archaeologists have been most interested in investigating. Some of the Maya cities or towns in this region that await further exploration are Aguateca, La Amelia, Dos Pilas, Tararindito, and El Caribe. Altar de Sacrificios, at the confluence of the Pasión and Salinas rivers, must have been an important trading center for the various peoples in the foothills of the river basin. It is possible that the merchants who controlled the trade on the rivers were members of ruling families from the major ceremonial centers adjacent to these waterways.

Luxury items such as jade, quetzal feathers, and obsidian from the Guatemala Highlands; salt and precious sea shells from the Pacific Slope; and ceramics from such cities as Chamá, Ratinlixul, and Zaculeu all came by the trade routes over the mountains and into the river systems of the Central and Southern Lowlands. Dur-

At Sayaxché this flat-top ferry, sometimes guided by dugout canoes, takes cars and passengers across the Pasión River. From here Seibal can be reached by dugout canoe or by a vehicle with four-wheel drive if the roads permit passage.

ing the Terminal Classic Period a ceramic ware called Fine Orange Ware was distributed widely from Campeche throughout the Lowlands. We can assume that the tropical Lowlands communities had specialized craft guilds to create the products in demand outside their own territories. Allspice, cacao, vanilla beans, and other luxury produce surely played an important role in trade. Markets at Seibal and Altar de Sacrificios must have been bustling trade centers.

The Pasión River area has a history of early occupation. At both Altar de Sacrificios and Seibal there is evidence of housing and pottery from as early as 900-600 B.C. At Seibal, Middle Preclassic pottery has been found under the hillock where the circular platform (Structure 79) stands in Group C. Both jade and obsidian were major imports in Late Preclassic times. Jade celts found in two caches excavated at Seibal resemble Olmec celts and may have been trade items from the Olmec area. Seibal continued to

175

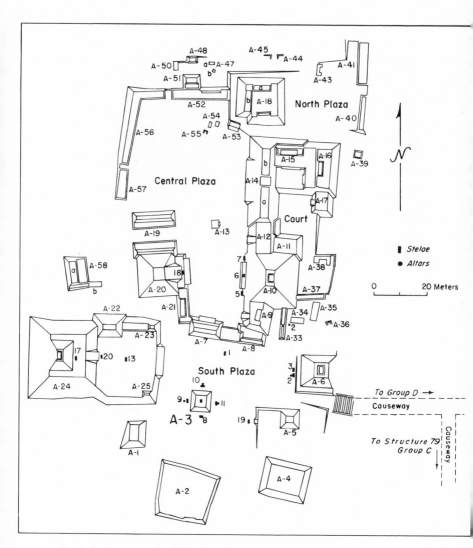

Seibal. After Ian Graham.

grow through the Late Preclassic Period, but during the Proto-classic Period it was partly abandoned. There is no indication of occupation between A.D. 500 and 690; the nature and cause of this hiatus are unknown. When the city was occupied again, a new era was ushered in.

During the Late Classic Period (A.D. 600–900) there was a burst of creative activity in the construction of buildings and monuments, and these are the structures we see today. Both Seibal and Altar de Sacrificios were highly influenced by non-Maya ideas during this period, an influence reflected in their sculpture and architecture. We see the use of speech scrolls, faces with straight noses and squared jaws, hair reaching to the waist, serpent motifs, and other ideas that were introduced from outside the Maya area. The carving on these monuments, however, was probably executed by skilled Maya sculptors. Fine Orange pottery found at both Seibal and Altar de Sacrificios indicates trade with the Gulf coast. Recent research suggests that the newcomers may have been Putun Maya from the Puuc or Chenes areas of Yucatán. In all probability their interest was control of the riverine and overland trade routes and markets. Later the Putun Maya abandoned the area for the more lucrative seagoing trade.

Seibal was at its peak in the Late Classic Period between A.D. 830 and 890. The population density was high on the periphery of the city, and dwellings with associated temple structures have been found as far as two miles away in the countryside. By 930 the city was again abandoned. During the next two centuries one Maya area after another—from the Pacific Slope into the Guatemala Highlands, the periphery of the Southern Lowlands, and finally the Maya Northern Lowlands of Yucatán—was abandoned or fell to invading groups from the Mexican area (Mexicanized Maya) on the north and west.

Today the heavy rainfalls in the Pasión Valley create a constant problem for the caretakers trying to keep the lush tropical forest from encroaching onto the monuments. Stelae are covered with lichens and algae. A brilliant orange alga has been especially persistent in covering the stelae, as seen on Stela 2. Seibal, situated on a low plateau, has a typical medium-sized ceremonial center,

Structure A-3 is the only structure at Seibal with a corbeled roof. Originally the plastered building was dark red. Although the ruins are very extensive, little of the site has been re-

stored. Seibal was occupied from Preclassic to Late Classic times, although it underwent a near hiatus during the Early Classic Period.

and the city is approximately one square mile in area. Temples and palacelike buildings are arranged around central courtyards and plazas, but they are not built on the grand scale of those at Tikal or Uaxactún. The plateau of Seibal is of limestone, a readily available building material. There are indications of two ball courts, one in Group A and the other in Group D. Causeways *(sacbeob)* connect the four major groups at Seibal (Groups A, B, C, and D), all on natural hilltops. Similar causeways are noted at the great ceremonial city Tikal, as well as at many other cities.

On first approaching the cleared area of the archaeological zone, one is a bit overwhelmed by the number of monuments to be seen. Only partial excavation and reconstruction have been carried out at Seibal. There are fifty-six stelae known to be here, twenty-two of which are uncarved, and the zone has twenty-two altars, most of them uncarved. The major group is Group A, dominated by a small temple known as Structure A-3, in the center of the South Plaza. Two other plazas are also associated with Group A, the Central Plaza and the North Plaza. In Group A are at least thirty building mounds buried under the jungle growth. Structure A-3 is the only completely restored structure here. The temple becomes increasingly important as one examines the four magnificent stelae, one on each side of this temple. In many ways the stelae resemble the recently discovered murals, also Terminal Classic, at Cacaxtla, in the state of Puebla, Mexico. Dates on the stelae at Seibal are all of the midninth century, which indicates that the temple is of the same period. When Willey and Smith excavated here, they reported a substructure that was used as a working platform to rebuild A-3. The front of Stela 9, on the west side of Structure A-3, is beautifully carved with a human figure, apparently a portrayal of a Putun Maya ruler, and glyphs, while the sides and

At the base of the stairway to Structure A-3 at Seibal is Stela 9. This Late Classic stela, as well as three others on each side of the building, bears the date corresponding to A.D. *849. During Late Classic times the Pasión River area was already coming under the influence and control of non-Maya groups intruding from the north.*

back are left plain. The flamboyant headdress with quetzal feathers places Stela 9 stylistically toward the close of the Late Classic Period. The glyphs have the date A.D. 849. The person on the monument holds a double-headed ceremonial bar decorated with constellation bands. Stelae 10 and 11 also depict personages — no doubt rulers — with many non-Mayan accoutrements. These sculptures are on the north and east sides of the same temple. Most of the sculptures at Seibal are a blend of the Maya style with elements from several other sources, including the Toltec and the Putun.

At the base of Temple A-3 many pieces of stucco and plaster have been found, indicating a rather extensive and rich decoration that must have been part of the cornice of the building. From an analysis of the stucco pieces found, it seems that an elaborate frieze with mythological figures, deities, animals, and human figures occupied the whole cornice. The frieze was painted in brilliant shades of red, blue, green, pink, black, and beige. It is possible that other buildings yet to be excavated may also contain handsome friezes. Some of the sculptures on this building were in low relief, while others were in high relief. Life-size human figures were evidently placed in the center of the cornice on each side of the building, stuccoed over stone armatures. This type of modeling is not unlike that of other Maya areas in which large figures were carved in stucco. Structure A-3 has a corbeled roof, the only one found to date at Seibal. The temple has three rooms, all connected by doorways. A stela and altar were found in the central room during excavation; they have been repaired and replaced in their original positions. The stela date, A.D. 849, is the same as that of the four stelae on the exterior of the temple.

A hieroglyphic stairway is at the base of Structure 14 in Group A. Hieroglyphic stairways have also been found at other sites, in-

In the village of Sayaxché, en route to Seibal, is Stela 2, a superb stela from La Amelia depicting a mighty ruler of Late Classic times. His unusual headdress, ear pendant, necklace, and leg bands are interesting adornments. A jaguar pedestal serves as the base.

Stela 13, at Seibal. This monument is unusual because of the many serpents that make up part of the ruler's ceremonial dress. The speech scroll, facial features, and costume indicate that the person is possibly a Putun Maya from northern Yucatán. Late Classic. Stone rubbing courtesy of Merle Green Robertson.

Stela 2, at Seibal, is non-Maya in style. The personage is a priest or ruler wearing a monkey mask and an elaborate headdress. Late Classic. In the wet, tropical jungles of the Petén it is not unusual to see stelae covered with bright-orange algae.

cluding Edzná, Quiriguá, Copán, Yaxchilán, and Palenque. The two palace structures at the top of the stairway may have been dwellings for important Seibal ruling families. Stela 13, a short distance from Structure A-3, is one of the most interesting stelae at Seibal. The important personage portrayed, possibly a ruler, is wearing beads, armbands, earplugs, anklets, and bracelets, all of jade. Around his waist is a handsomely carved serpent tied in a great bow, representing the belt of his ceremonial dress. Six additional serpents projecting from the sides of the skirt are similar in design to the reliefs on the Tzompantli structure at Chichén Itzá. The facial features, speech scrolls, serpent forms, and costume detail on this stela suggest that the person depicted was a Putun Maya ruler who was well aware of his cultural heritage and who may have been from the northern Yucatán area.

The only monument at Seibal with a standing figure facing forward, who also has his face forward rather than in profile, is Stela 2. Full-faced stela figures are more common at Piedras Negras, Copán, and Quiriguá. Stela 2 has no carved glyphs, which is unusual. The person depicted on the monument may be a deity or a priest representing a deity, for he wears a mask on his face, and his headdress is formed by a large death's-head.

Group D is the largest of the four sections at Seibal; it has more than fifty building mounds. Few carved monuments are found here, however; most are in the area of Group A. The visitor can take long walks on footpaths at Seibal, going from one group to another, and see many stelae and mounds of unexcavated buildings. A good hike along one of the forest trails southeast of Group A brings the visitor to Group C. The trail follows Causeway I and Causeway II, which were great *sacbeob* when Seibal was active in Late Classic times. There has been very little excavation in the area, and mounds can be seen covered with rich tropical vegetation indicating sites of various unexcavated monuments.

Unique in this area is a large reconstructed circular platform known as Structure 79, which is approached by a *sacbé*. The platform is composed of three terraces with a major stairway on the west side. On the east side is another small stairway. A rectangular raised platform on the top of Structure 79 could have been a base

Structure 79, at Seibal. This restored circular platform was the foundation for a temple that has long since perished. The circular shape was rarely used by the Maya. An influence from the Mexican area is noted in this structure. Late Classic.

for a small pole-and-thatch temple. Excavation under this structure revealed a rectangular platform from an earlier era, suggesting that the area was in continued use for a long time. On the west side of Structure 79 is the Jaguar Altar, circular in design and supported by three pedestals, two of which are carved with crouching figures. A crude jaguar is carved on the side of the altar in a style similar to that noted at the Toltec capital, Tula. The glyph date, however, is A.D. 870, much earlier than that of the Toltec city.

Even after four seasons of archaeological work, most of Seibal and its history lie buried far below the ground. Nevertheless, what is now visible is of substantial aid in piecing together Maya history. It is too great a task to uncover all the Maya cities, but each archaeological expedition unfolds more information about the Maya and their remarkable civilization.

7   The Guatemala Highlands: Kaminaljuyú, Zaculeu, Mixco Viejo, and Iximché

Kaminaljuyú

The Guatemala Highlands, a rugged mountain range stretching from the Mexican border to El Salvador, encompasses some of the most beautiful scenic territory in all of Central America. Volcanic peaks, some of them active, are reflected in the many lakes along the range. Present-day Maya villages have maintained an economy, an architecture, and a way of life that have changed little since the Spanish conquest. The regional dress of the Maya is by far the most colorful in the Americas. Clothing must be warm, especially during the chilly winter nights, when frost can occasionally be seen in the villages high in the mountains. The altitude of most of the villages is between 4,500 and 6,500 feet.

Even though burros are now sometimes used as beasts of burden, one is more likely to see heavy loads supported by tumplines and carried on the backs of the Maya walking up and down the mountain trails and roadways. The Maya are a stocky, sturdy people, proud of their families, their villages, and their heritage.

The Guatemala Highlands have been the home of the Maya since Preclassic times. Many cities here reached an apogee early in Maya civilization, while others are of a very late Postclassic date. There are more than one hundred archaeological sites, only a few of which have been uncovered.

Construction began at Kaminaljuyú in Preclassic times, and by the end of that era a large city had been established. Over three hundred mounds and thirteen ball courts, all built of adobe, date from this period. During the Late Preclassic Period sculpture and pottery reached a level of development unequaled by any other area of the Highlands. Large stone carvings found here are reminiscent of Izapa-style sculptures, well known along the Pacific Slope

188

and in southern Mexico. Sculptured boulders similar to some of those found at Monte Alto suggest even earlier activity at the ceremonial center at Kaminaljuyú, possibly as early as the Middle Preclassic Period (800–300 B.C.). At the end of the Late Preclassic Period the city was abandoned.

During the Early Classic Period (A.D. 300–600), Kaminaljuyú was active again. At this time the city came under the influence of Teotihuacán peoples from the mountains of Mexico, who may have conquered the city. These intrusive peoples were probably interested in gaining control of the trade routes and possibly of the sources of minerals such as obsidian and jade in the Highlands. They also filtered into the Pacific Slope and no doubt controlled the cacao and cotton plantations. Their influence is especially noticeable in the architecture and pottery at Kaminaljuyú. Building stones were carefully cut pumice set in an adobe mortar and then plastered and painted. Because such perishable materials were used, especially the adobe, little remains to be seen at Kaminaljuyú today except dirt mounds and underground tunnels made by archaeologists for strata tests and preliminary excavations. Guatemala City now encompasses most of the existing mounds. From the ruins of Kaminaljuyú, the largest Maya site in the Highlands, a tremendous number of artifacts—especially pottery, jade, pyrite plaques, and many other objects in caches—have been recovered. Some of these objects bear stylistic similarities to those of the Classic Veracruz culture, especially the pyrite-encrusted plaques and the stone sculptures associated with the ball game. At the end of the Early Classic Period Kaminaljuyú, once a city with a maximum population of 50,000, was again abandoned, at the same time that Teotihuacán, in Mexico, collapsed.

During Late Classic times no important ceremonial centers were built in the Guatemala Highlands. At this time the flowering of the Maya civilization had its impact in the Southern Lowlands at such sites as Tikal, Piedras Negras, and Yaxchilán. Copán and Quiriguá retained their power in the southern extremities of the Lowlands during Late Classic times, while Uxmal, Sayil, Labná, and Kabah reached an apogee in the Puuc Hills of Yucatán, in the Northern Lowlands.

189

Kaminaljuyú, an extremely important commercial center during the Late Preclassic and Early Classic periods. Since most of the center was constructed of adobe and pumice, little of Kaminaljuyú remains to be seen today. Most of the excavations are underground in tunnels. The mounds visible in the

foreground are still unexcavated. Footpaths lead to various sections where excavation has been in progress. In the distance is Guatemala City, which has expanded over a large part of the Kaminaljuyú site.

Zaculeu

Zaculeu, a compact ceremonial center approximately two miles from Huehuetenango, was restored in 1946-47 under the auspices of the United Fruit Company. Richard B. Woodbury and Aubrey S. Trik recorded the excavations and restorations here. This ceremonial center, like many others in the Guatemala Highlands, is not outstanding in architecture or monumental sculpture when compared with the Lowland Maya cities. In Classic times both Zaculeu and Nebaj were contemporary with Kaminaljuyú and had certain characteristics in common. Their craftsmen executed some of the finest pyrite plaques and jade carvings in the Maya area. Zaculeu, the capital city of the Mam Maya, who occupied the western Highlands of Guatemala, and Nebaj continued to be active throughout the Postclassic Period and up to the Spanish conquest.

Set in the Huehuetenango Valley, the archaeological site of Zaculeu is surrounded by misty mountain ranges that spread a soft green veil over the entire countryside. The elevation is 6,500 feet, and warm clothing and well-built dwellings are required. Frost is not uncommon. The valley is fertile and has enough rainfall to permit two corn crops a year. The topsoil is dark and loamy and rests on a subsoil of clay, a great asset for adobe construction. At one time this mountainous area was heavily forested, but the forests have been cut back; they are now controlled by the government to ensure the provision of sufficient wood for the Maya to build their houses and to use for fuel. Just west of the ceremonial center is a small stream, the Río Selegua, which provides the water needed by the farmers. Unfortunately, no study has been made of the house mounds of pre-Conquest times; such a study would enable archaeologists to determine the population pattern and density of the area. Valleys and sloping hills were most likely used for village compounds, much as they are today. Over the centuries Mexicanized Maya moved into the Highlands and brought with them many cultural elements that are readily noticeable in the architecture and artifacts of Postclassic times.

During Captain Pedro de Alvarado's conquest of Guatemala, Zaculeu was one of many small centers that came under his ruthless attack. The Spaniard was merciless in his attempts to take the town. The Maya, on foot and using bows and arrows, were no match for the Spaniards on their horses and armed with guns. Under the chief Caibil Balam the Zaculeu Maya finally had to surrender in 1525. Nevertheless, they showed great fortitude in holding off the Spaniards for several months before they were forced to surrender.

The restored portion of the Zaculeu ceremonial center is not very large, and the architecture is extremely plain. There are,

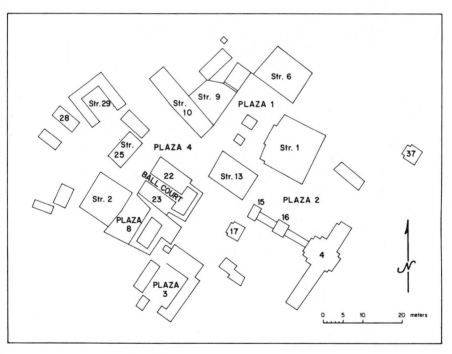

Zaculeu. After Dimick.

Structure 1, which dominated the Main Plaza at Zaculeu. This temple structure is the highest one here. In the foreground are two small platforms that may have been used for dance, oratory, or music. Such structures were used during Postclassic times.

however, pleasing variations in the shapes of buildings, in the platforms supporting superstructures, and in the placement of buildings. Little alignment to the cardinal points, a feature of most Classic sites, is evident here. There are no indications of the roof combs, moldings, bas-reliefs, stucco-decorated piers, or corbeled vaults common at other Maya cities. Of the many buildings excavated so far, only Structure 13 bears any evidence of painted plaster. As many as twelve superimpositions have been discovered at Zaculeu, indicating construction from the end of Early Classic times until the Conquest. In all there are forty-three structures at Zaculeu arranged around plazas and courtyards.

Structure 1 is an impressive temple and is the largest building here. It contains seven superimpositions and reaches a height of

Structure 13, at Zaculeu, may have been used as a ceremonial chamber or as a residence for the elite. The ball court can be seen in the distance. After the buildings were restored, they were painted white, although the original color of paint was quite different.

just over thirty-nine feet. Because the time allotted for the reconstruction of Zaculeu was relatively short for such an undertaking, little excavation could be done. Trenches dug by archaeologists into the interior of the structure indicate the number of superimpositions. The façade of the last superimposition on Structure 1 has eight terraces and is broken by a double stairway with a medial ramp on the five lower terraces. Two square columns support the three doorways of the temple. Both round and square columns were used on façades of structures of Zaculeu.

The best-preserved building at Zaculeu is Structure 4, an unusually long building with north and south wings. A pillared portico running the length of the structure and the benches along the wall at the rear suggest that the building could have been used for the review of festivals and ceremonies in the adjoining plaza (Plaza 2). A similar type of porticoed gallery is found in Plaza 4 (Structure 10). This singularly long building could also have been used by

195

the ruling elite as a vantage point to watch festivals, dances, musicals, or religious ceremonies.

Structure 13 faces Plaza 1 and may have been a temple building, since it has only a single room that is hardly suitable for habitation. Five superimpositions have been counted under this structure, the final one constructed just before the Spanish conquest. The building is architecturally the most distinctive at the site. Bands of green, red, and blue paint can be seen on the piers between the doorways.

The ball court, which has been reconstructed, is small. While it lacks the usual Postclassic rings or markers used for the game, these could have been painted directly onto the plaster benches and the alley of the court. Superstructures were placed on either side of the court, like those at Copán, but only the foundations are here today, giving us little indication of their function or even their exact dimensions. In a deeper excavation into the ball court, an earlier, smaller court was discovered under the present one.

From the great number of burials and caches excavated at Zaculeu, much can be learned about burial customs, home industries, trade items, and the chronology of artifacts. Excavations carried out at the sites of Nebaj, Chamá, and Ratinlixul, all of which lie northeast of the Zaculeu mountain range, have also produced a wealth of material that gives us better insight into the daily life of the times. The superb paintings on the Late Classic pottery at Chamá and Ratinlixul are in narrative form, showing many scenes of the ceremonial life of the people, their mythology, and religious ceremonies. Because of their proximity to the Petén area they are related stylistically to the Maya Lowland pottery rather than to that of the Guatemala Highlands. The brilliant brush strokes, sometimes made with feathers, depict the physical contours of the Maya lords and other classes of peoples. The artistry reached a zenith in the Chamá vases, the masterpieces of this great civilization.

At Zaculeu there was only one really great burial tomb, and that was under Structure 1, the major temple here. Burial practices at Zaculeu varied greatly. Bodies were interned in vaults, cists, and urns, and cremation became common toward the end of the period. There were no particular burial customs related to age or sex, and bodies were buried in both extended and flexed positions. The extended position was more widely used in the beginning of the Late Classic Period. Urn burials at Zaculeu apparently took place exclusively in Postclassic times, but so far only six have been found here. The urns were cut at the top to allow the body to be placed inside in a flexed position; then the urn was covered and tied together. Human sacrifice was practiced; this becomes evident from the remains of the victims found in the graves of important persons. The kinds of burials in Zaculeu can be seen in the little museum adjoining the archaeological zone.

Plaques of pyrite mounted on slate backs have been found in great numbers at Zaculeu, Kaminaljuyú, and Nebaj. Thirty-three of these plaques were found in Structure 1 at Zaculeu. Plaques of this type have a wide distribution, and the Guatemala Highlands may have been the center of the industry. The craftsmanship involved in making a plaque is technically remarkable. Pyrite is a very hard mineral, as hard as jade. The difficulty in working with pyrite is its lack of cohesion; it has a tendency to crumble. For this reason the surfaces of the plaques are mosaics made of small pieces of pyrite cut and fitted together. On some of the plaques the mosaic lines are so accurate that they are hardly discernible. The pyrite takes on a very high metallic polish that can be blinding in the sun. Perforations on either side of the plaques indicate that they were suspended from the neck and worn by chiefs or priests on ceremonial occasions. They may have had magical or religious significance. Because of the uneven surface of the plaques it is hardly possible they were used as mirrors. Not too many of these plaques have been found in good condition, for oxidization tends to disintegrate the mineral. Some of the slate backs on which the pyrite was mounted, however, are carved in beautiful relief designs, many of them in the Classic Veracruz style. Many of the ceremonial centers of the Guatemala Highlands were influenced first by Teotihuacán in the Early Classic Period and later by Veracruz in the Late Classic Period, typified by the site El Tajín.

Although gold and metal alloys were made into objects of great beauty in South America as early as the Late Preclassic Period, metals and the techniques of working with them did not reach

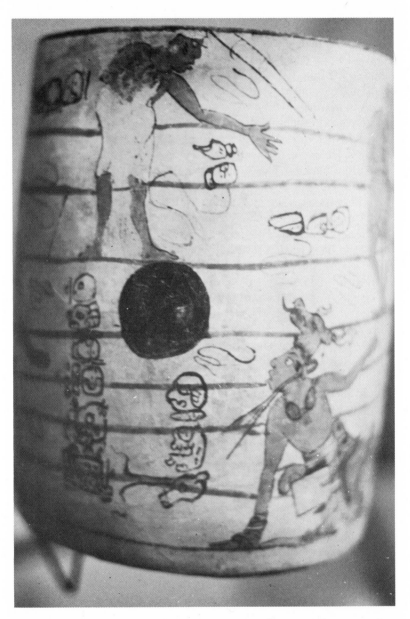

These narrative ceramics, depicting ceremonial scenes, deities, and the elite of Maya society, represent a most important phase of ceramic-ware development during Late Classic times. This particular narrative

scene portrays a ball game in action. Courtesy American Museum of Natural History.

Mesoamerica until Postclassic times. Most of the Maya area has limestone, in which no metals are found. Gold and copper objects found at Zaculeu were probably trade pieces from Panama or Costa Rica. Metal objects as well as Plumbate pottery have been found in burials at this archaeological site.

Although some jade pieces were found in both caches and burials at Zaculeu, they were not of the quality noted in Kaminaljuyú or Nebaj, the great jade centers. Nebaj is the only Maya site that has been scientifically excavated to arrive at a chronology of jade styles. Some of the finest pieces of Maya jade were carved here, and, indeed, Nebaj may have been a center for the industry. Sources of jade have been found at Manzanal, and jade boulders, stones, and pebbles are known to have been recovered from the Motagua River. There probably were other sources in the Guatemala Highlands in Classic times, but they were soon depleted and have been long forgotten. Some magnificent jades have also been found at Tikal, Palenque, and Toniná, in Chiapas. A few pieces are carved in narrative relief.

There are stylistic differences in Early and Late Classic jades. In particular, Early Classic jades were designed to retain the shape of the original stone. At that time both the low and the high sections of the carving were polished. Facial lines were more symbolic than realistic. Carving of the Late Classic Period takes on a very crisp relief, with polishing confined mostly to the upper surface. The execution of the body and facial expressions is more relaxed and naturalistic. Nebaj jade is distinguished by a mottling of green and light gray. Jade pieces found at Kaminaljuyú and Toniná are more likely to be emerald green or apple green.

There are many similarities between the Zaculeu site and Nebaj, even though they are separated by a mountain range. Their methods of burial, their crafts, and their chronology have parallels. It is quite possible that Zaculeu was an important trading center for the Maya en route from the tributaries of the Usumacinta River to the Pacific Slope. Nebaj was influenced by the art styles along the Usumacinta. Zaculeu in turn came under the influence of Nebaj craftsmen, but the Zaculeu Maya retained certain regional traits more closely related to the adjacent Guatemala Highland cere-

This seated Maya figure is one of a group of jades found in a single burial at Toniná, Chiapas. The use of the tube drill for the circular lines, the carving of the figure and the background on two planes, and the general characteristics of the facial features identify this jade as Late Classic. Courtesy American Museum of Natural History.

monial centers. Trade routes were important to the Maya for the exchange of ideas, the spread of culture, and the advancement of learning. Paramount to the Maya, however, was the economic value in terms of management control. Ultimately the routes were utilized for advancing Mexican migrations and Spanish conquistadors.

Mixco Viejo

Traveling north from Guatemala City to Mixco Viejo, one has an opportunity to pass through remote Maya villages and hillside towns that are not on the usual visitor's itinerary. Vegetable and flower gardens terraced on the mountainsides provide produce for markets

201

in Guatemala City, just an hour or two away. There is a hazard in trying to reach Mixco Viejo by car: one must cross a tributary of the Motagua River. Sometimes the bridge is out because of flooding or earthquakes, and the car may have to be driven through the river. If the water is too deep, there is a chance that the car will stall partway across.

Approximately two miles beyond the bridge the distant horizon silhouettes the temple platform of Mixco Viejo. During the dry season golden-brown grasses soften the hilltops and cast mauve shadows that darken the rugged ravines. Mixco Viejo stands on the top of a rugged promontory in the Chimaltenango district of Guatemala, an ideal location for a fortified city. There are more than 120 major structures here, including temple and palace platforms, altars, ball courts, and many subsidiary buildings that may have served any number of purposes. At the time of the Spanish conquest perhaps as many as ten thousand Pokomam Maya lived on the surrounding mountainsides and paid tribute to the Pokomam chiefs. This mountaintop city, like others, was an extremely important military fortress, trading center, and dwelling place for the chiefs, the military, and their families.

Mixco Viejo, like Iximché, is a Late Postclassic site and probably has a history going back no earlier than the thirteenth century. Many chiefs of Mixco Viejo claimed descent from the Mexicanized Maya, and indeed their cities reflect the Toltec-Aztec type of architecture. The city was destroyed by Pedro de Alvarado, the Spanish general who burned all the local villages and dispersed the population. The Pokomam Maya never regained power.

On approaching the ruins of Mixco Viejo today, one can appreciate the wisdom of the Maya in selecting this mountaintop for their city. A grand vista of the surrounding countryside can be seen in all directions. The building program at the site was extensive, and the natural terrain, with many ravines, was a factor in the placement of temples and other structures. The similarity in the architectural style to that of the Toltecs and Aztecs of Mexico is not unique to Mixco Viejo. Mexican influence is visible in all the fortified cities of the Highlands. The platform bases of various structures have divided stairways separated by medial ramps and

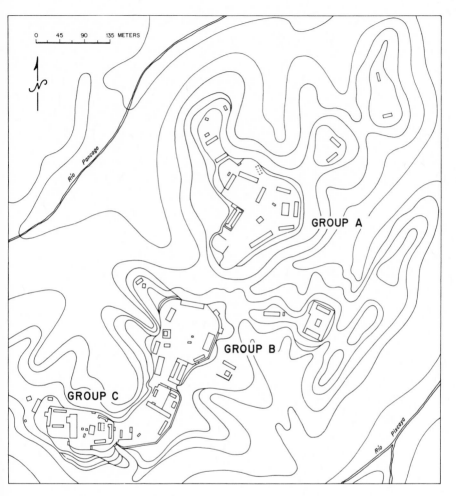

Mixco Viejo. After Smith.

Mixco Viejo, situated on top of a steep hill in the Guatemala High-lands. Only a portion of the city can be seen. The site was an impor-tant one in Postclassic times as a fortification of the Pokomam Maya. There are many multichambered structures here, including palacelike structures, twin temples, altar platforms, and ball courts.

flanked by balustrades. As in Aztec architecture, the construction of twin temples on a single pyramid was also in vogue at Mixco Viejo. Twin temples once stood on Pyramid B-3 in Group B, north of the ball court. The five terraces of the pyramid are diminutive, and the ramps on either side of the staircase are nearly as wide as the stairs. Today little remains of the two temples. There is a small altar at the base of each staircase.

The sunken ball court in Group B, similar to that at Tula, is adjacent to the major plaza and is the best preserved court here. Instead of the usual ring marker on the sidewalls of the court, a carved serpent holding a human head in its gaping mouth was the marker for the ball game. The only original marker found here was removed to the museum in Guatemala City. The court was reconstructed with cement replicas of the original marker.

The restored sunken ball court at Mixco Viejo was in the shape of a capital I, *was stuccoed and painted, and contained serpent heads on the walls on either side of the playing alley. The serpent heads here today are replicas; the only original marker found is now in the museum in Guatemala City.*

Another sunken ball court, whose sidewalls and floor are covered with the original stucco, is found in Group A, near the north end of the ceremonial center. Deep ravines separate this group of buildings from other areas of the hilltop site. Here, as in all other parts of this fortified city, the buildings have no particular orientation but are clustered according to the irregular terrain of the hilltop. The builders carefully planned drainage systems for courts and plazas to ensure suitable areas for military maneuvers and for living quarters. In the light of the secular trend evident in these late ceremonial centers, the platforms in these courts and plazas

205

may have been used for entertainment as well as religious and court ceremonies, and they may also have served other functions. It is even possible that the original use of the plazas for religious functions and pilgrimages may have been replaced in Postclassic times with commercial use as marketplaces. The new cities that flourished at this late date may well have been administrative centers and capitals for warring regional groups. As Mixco Viejo grew into a fair-sized city, protective walls were constructed, and buildings were enlarged for the increasing population. The many superimpositions within the buildings at Mixco Viejo today can be seen from underground tunnels.

Between 1954 and 1967, Henri Lehmann, director of the Franco-Guatemalan Archaeological Mission, carried out systematic excavations here and discovered large quantities of funerary urns, incense burners, and many other ceramics. Funerary urns were important, since cremation was popular at Mixco Viejo and at many other hilltop sites during Postclassic times.

Buildings were stuccoed and painted, but no reliefs or other decorations are evident. Group C was probably the most important group on this hilltop, and it can be seen from any point in the surrounding valleys. The structures are still covered with a thick coating of white stucco, but fragments show that they were originally painted. Pyramid C-1 is the most impressive building on this side of the ceremonial center; it has three superimpositions easily seen by the visitor.

Funerary deposits in Group C included a copper ax and a string of gold bells. Offerings placed in ceramic bowls were present at most burials. It is not unusual to find metal objects dating from Late Postclassic times at the ceremonial centers. These objects were probably imported into the area from Mexico, an important source of metals.

Today Mixco Viejo sleeps quietly in the beautiful countryside of Chimaltenango. Those who undertake the journey to the site are impressed by the grand vistas to be seen from the mountaintops of the rugged country, by the remoteness of the ruins from the usual Maya workaday world, and by the way the rural Maya of today still adhere to the old traditions.

Of the many (over one hundred) structures at Mixco Viejo, this building, called Pyramid C-1, is one of the few still showing remains of plaster applied in the fifteenth century. There is no decoration on the building except the painted plaster. The style is Postclassic.

Iximché

During Postclassic times Maya cities in the Guatemalan Highlands such as Iximché, Mixco Viejo, and Zaculeu were in a state of constant change until the Spanish conquest. This was a period of strife for the Maya and a time when regional chiefs were competing for power. Hereditary ruling families were seeking legitimacy by claiming descent from Toltec or Mexicanized Maya families. To expand their territory and increase their tribute from both the local people and those scattered in villages far into the countryside, the rulers usually maintained a constant state of war to procure slaves as well as persons for sacrifice. Invading migrant groups from the Valley of Mexico, northern Yucatán, or the Pacific Slope were also seeking new territory and creating other problems. This modus operandi continued over a long period of time. The precedent for this kind of expansion took place along the Pacific Slope in Middle Preclassic times and in the Pasión River district during the Terminal Classic Period. As the Maya civilization began to erode during the ninth and tenth centuries, Mexicanized Maya peoples moved into the old Maya territories, bringing with them new ideas that were to replace the traditional Maya way of life.

By late Postclassic times the Aztecs were conquering all the territory surrounding their domain and demanding tribute from areas as far south as Guatemala. Moctezuma had been receiving tribute from Iximché for many years and was considering expanding Aztec territory into the Caribbean islands as well. Introduction of non-Maya cultural patterns and ideas into architecture, religion, ceremonies, and warfare was effective in varying degrees.

In the Guatemala Highlands civic centers had to be fortified to serve as places of refuge during wars. New fortified cities were built on mountaintops rather than in valleys. Because of the disruptive intrusions development in the arts regressed considerably. Architecture was no longer on the grand scale, sculpture was no longer of distinction, and little pottery was made for other than utilitarian purposes. Ceremonial centers became more secularized and served different functions, depending on the particular interests of local and regional chiefs. Village life, accordingly, varied considerably from one area to another, reflecting the political unrest, the changing religious patterns, and the economic uncertainties of the times.

In the Highlands hamlets in the mountainous areas were self-sustaining and had little need for contact with larger centers. Farming villages were common in the valleys and on the slopes of mountains where the water supply was adequate for agriculture and daily household use. Larger towns were more cosmopolitan and were closely related to the activities of the ceremonial-civic centers of the region. Such towns were bustling with trade and industry. Items from the Highlands such as salt, quetzal feathers, jade, and obsidian were exported. In Postclassic times copper axes and other metal objects, some made of gold, were imported from the Mexican area.

Lineage was exceedingly important in controlling Maya society. Civic leaders, priests, craftsmen, merchants, and farmers had inherited rights that were passed down from one generation to another. There was apparently little opportunity to change social status in Maya society. Spanish chronicles indicate that this was especially true at the hilltop site Iximché.

Iximché is in the central Highland mountain and lake district a short distance from Lake Atitlán. Until 1524 it was the capital city of the Cakchiqué Maya. The present-day village nearest the ruins is Tecpán. Iximché was built approximately half a century before the Spanish conquest. It has a fairly large civic center surrounded for the most part by deep ravines and dry moats for defense.

Most of the buildings were erected around four large courtyards. There are also two smaller courtyards at Iximché that may have been used for religious ceremonies. Terraces were leveled from the natural terrain to accommodate platforms for temples, palaces, and other structures. The structures had roofs of thatch or of wooden beams and plaster and have long since perished. Ball courts were common at all civic and religious centers. At Iximché there are two ball courts one of which, Ballcourt 8, has been restored. The sunken court is of medium size and has vertical playing walls and stairways at either end for use by the players.

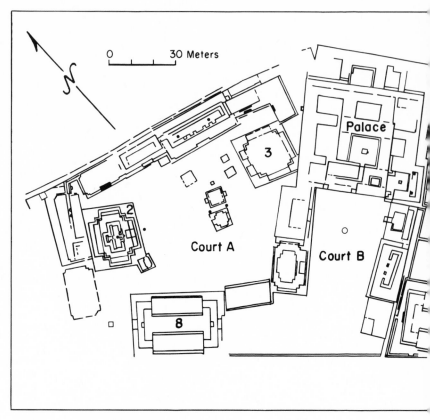

Iximché. After Guillemin.

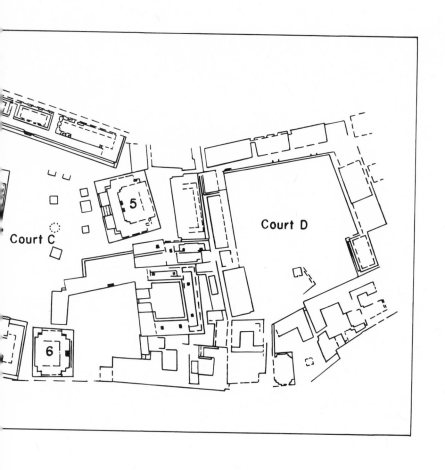

Court A, Iximché. In the foreground are platforms for two small altars. At the left is the platform of Temple III. Behind and at the right of Temple III can be seen the foundation of the great palace and its adjoining Court B. Postclassic.

Court alleys were slightly slanted for water drainage. Ditches were then used to channel the water down into the ravines. Most ball courts were drained in a similar manner throughout Mesoamerica. The builders of Iximché provided additional drainage facilities for the courts and patios of the various structures.

Important buildings such as those clustered around Courts A and C were constructed of stone and mortar and were then plastered and painted. Superstructures were of perishable materials such as adobe or wood. All the plazas and courtyards were plastered and painted, a practice that was renewed at the death of each chief. At that time also tribute in the form of ceramics, sculptures, and labor was paid to the family of the dead ruler so that new structures could be built in honor of the new chief. Three superimpositions are noted in Temple 2 as well as in the adjoining Court A. This temple was still in use when the Spaniards

The ball court in Court A, at Iximché, is one of two known courts at this site. Courts of this period usually had closed ends and vertical sides.

conquered the area. Since then some of the buildings have been demolished and the stones used for local construction, as can be seen in Tecpán.

Of the four courts, A and C are enclosed with similar structures. On the north side of each court is a platform that supported three structures, possibly residences or administrative buildings. Each court has two temples facing each other (Temples 2, 3, 4, and 5) and altars in the plaza areas. Courts A and C were no doubt used for important ceremonials. Court B must have been a sanctuary for the occupants of the great palace structure northeast of the court plaza. Court D also must have been mainly a residential area for the families of the elite members of the city. There are not as many structures here, however, and they are smaller than those at the other three courts.

213

Temple 2 contains wall murals, now in very poor condition, executed in a manner highly reminiscent of the painting style noted in Mixtec codices. According to George F. Guillemin, who excavated here, there is evidence of murals in several other structures as well. The Mixtec and the Aztec in the Valley of Mexico and the peoples they influenced were great transporters of their art, culture, and religion to many ceremonial centers throughout Mesoamerica during Postclassic times. Such sites as Tulum and Santa Rita Corozal came under their influence.

In most structures at Iximché benches are common and served as seats. In Temple 2 of Court A were found a great number of ceramic incense burners typical of those used in the Highlands in Postclassic times. Cinnamon-colored cups used at Zaculeu and Mixco Viejo were also in use here. Since white-on-red ceramics (white paint on a red clay base) are also abundant, one can assume that the chronology fits comfortably into the Late Postclassic Period. Although sculpture is rare, two-legged stone metates and objects of jade and obsidian have been excavated.

Offerings of decapitated heads and obsidian knives have been found at Iximché, suggesting the importance of war and human sacrifice at this time. Slaves obtained from battle were an important labor force for the ceremonial centers.

At Iximché most of the dead were buried under buildings, the bodies being placed in a flexed position. In one such burial were found the remains of an important personage adorned with a simple gold crown, gold beads, and a bracelet of carved bone, ornaments not too different in style from those found in the Mixtec Tomb 7 at Monte Alban. Although gold as a trade item has been found in some Postclassic Maya sites, it is rare.

Iximché did not have an architecturally important ceremonial center, nor did it produce any outstanding works of art. The community and its fortified center were typical of the many hilltop towns of this period. The structures and platforms at Iximché and Mixco Viejo are quite similar in style, reflecting the strong Mexican influence of the time. The haste with which they were built shows little regard for traditional Maya arts and reflects the unsettled political situation before the Spanish conquest.

8 The Puuc Hills and Campeche: Uxmal, Kabáh, Sayil, Xlapak, Labná, and Edzna

Uxmal

In its prehistory a large part of Central America and Mexico, including the Yucatán Peninsula, was submerged beneath the sea. Because Yucatán is a shelf of porous limestone, lakes and rivers are virtually nonexistent. The only sources of fresh water on the northern coast are subterranean water systems called cenotes. The famed Well of Sacrifice at Chichén Itzá is one of these cenotes. Rain is rare from the first of the year until late May; in fact, in Yucatán rain is most welcome the year round. The Maya population density increases in areas where cenotes are present, because there the Maya can have wells in their compounds.

Farther south in Yucatán, in the Puuc Hills, there are no cenotes. Farmers there rely on reservoirs called chultunes that collect the rainwater. Chultunes are large, bottle-shaped cisterns which the ancient Maya either dug out of the limestone or built into the second stories of palace buildings. After the chultun had been shaped, it was given a very thick coat of plaster, often an inch thick, so that it would retain the rainwater. Good examples of the two types of cisterns can be seen at ground level behind the palace at Sayil and on the second story of the palace building at Labná. Neither site is far from Uxmal.

The Puuc Hills rise so gradually on the drive from Mérida to Uxmal that one is hardly aware of the change in altitude from sea level to 350 feet, except for the slightly cooler air, which is refreshing after the heat of Mérida. The Hacienda Uxmal is one of the most pleasant hotels in all of Yucatán, and the archaeological ruins, covering over 250 acres, are just a few hundred yards away.

Dynastic rule was as important to the Maya of Yucatán as it was to those of the Southern Lowlands. From epigraphic data we learn that a Maya dynasty governed the Uxmal area during Late

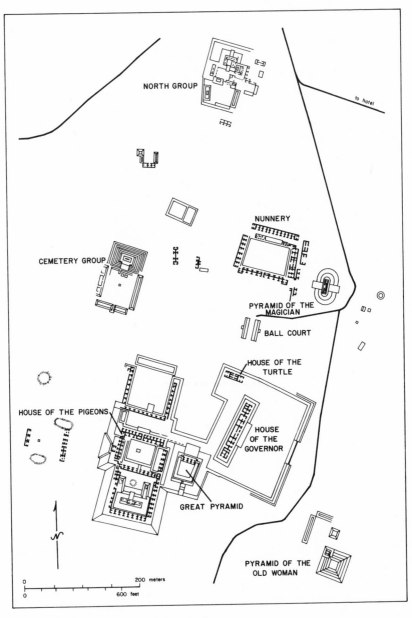

Uxmal. After Morley and Brainerd.

Classic times. This dynasty may have been related to other ruling families at Kabáh, Sayil, and Labná. Considering the frequent use of Puuc architectural style in Chichén Itzá and Dzibilchaltún, however, it is quite possible that a political alliance existed between these areas as well. An overland trade network through these cities may have been an economic factor in maintaining close ties. In Terminal Classic times these cities had strong affiliations with the Putun Maya, who set up new routes that expanded trade into the Caribbean and up riverine regions of what are now Honduras, Belize, and Guatemala. It is probable that along with this expansion came colonization.

The master plan for the city and ceremonial center of Uxmal is in marked contrast to the Lowland Maya sites in the Petén or along the Usumacinta River. The architects were revolutionary in their design. This spacious, open, flat terrain suggested new possibilities to them. Buildings were constructed on extremely large platforms, well spaced from one another. The plazas covered extensive areas of the ceremonial center. The architectonic relationship between the vertical masses of the pyramids and the horizontal masses of the low-lying palace and nunnerylike structures shows great harmony with space and with the natural environment. The heavy piers used in the Lowlands were replaced here with round and square columns, allowing much more light into rooms. Cut stone decorated with stucco was abandoned in favor of a new method of construction: instead of solid-core walls, the builders in Yucatán used a rubble core faced with clean-cut mosaic stone.

The mosaic-stone designs are usually geometric; naturalistic shapes, however, such as those of serpents, turtles, masks, and human beings, are incorporated into the geometric patterns. The Maya of Uxmal were not the only group using mosaic cut stones in geometric patterns for the façades of buildings in Late Classic times. At El Tajín, in Veracruz, buildings were decorated with mosaic-stone patterns, and in Postclassic times the Mixtec, who built the palace structure at Mitla, used a similar decoration lavishly. The Maya at Uxmal, however, developed the style to its perfection.

Mansard roofs, popular in the Usumacinta region, were rarely constructed in the Puuc Hills. One possible exception is the Palace

The great plaza area between the House of the Governor and the Nunnery Quadrangle at Uxmal. The city was built during the Late Classic Period.

at Kabáh, the modified cornice of which is battered, creating a mansardlike look. For their buildings the Maya in the Puuc Hills preferred vertical walls with the façade above the medial molding decorated with mosaic patterns and the stone wall below left plain. In the development of the cornice, attention was given to forms more varied than those of any other Maya site in Mesoamerica. Some of these architectural styles were also used in the Río Bec, Chenes, Puuc, and Chichén Itzá areas of Yucatán. The culmination of the Puuc style, seen at Uxmal, Kabáh, Sayil, and Labná, developed through centuries of progressive artistic development.

In the Northern Lowlands stelae were apparently erected only at Cobá and Uxmal. The remains of fifteen eroded stelae were found on a platform west of the Nunnery at Uxmal. There is also a stela in the Nunnery quadrangle on the stairs to the North Building. The calendar system using the Long Count, the most accurate of the Maya systems of recording time, was also abandoned. Such changes as these suggest a swing from a traditional, historical culture based on complex religious and mathematical systems to a transitional culture in which many of the old systems were discarded and the social mores underwent radical changes. On the other hand, possible astronomical alignments at Uxmal at the House of the Magicians, the Cemetery group, and the House of the Old Woman suggest that there was no disruption in the science of astronomy.

Uxmal was constructed during the Late Classic Period and reached an apogee between A.D. 800 and 1000. Since no systematic archaeological investigations have been conducted here, the length of occupation before and after that period is undocumented. Much restoration has been carried out by Mexican archaeologists, however. The name of one ruler is recorded on an altar south of the House of the Governor, that of Lord Chac and his parents, Chac Uinal Kan and Lady Bone. Their names also appear on a capstone in the Nunnery with the date equivalent to A.D. 907. The Uxmal emblem glyph has been tentatively identified in inscriptions at Uxmal. Because of the paucity of epigraphs as well as the erosion on stelae, there is little evidence to substantiate the historical development here.

The east façade of the House of the Magician, Uxmal, with the great stairway to Temple V. This unusual-shaped pyramid-temple complex has five superimpositions. Temple V, which rests on the top of Temple III, was the last superimposition. The House of the Magician is ninety-three feet high.

An old Maya legend tells of an elderly witch who hatched a child from an egg. After a year the child had developed into a dwarf with supernatural powers. Challenged by the Lord of Uxmal to build a temple in one night or face death, the dwarf succeeded in this task (as well as in others), and ultimately he himself became the Lord of Uxmal. The Great Pyramid at Uxmal is supposed to have been built by him and for this reason is called the House of the Magician. It is the tallest pyramid structure here, rising to ninety-three feet. The oldest pyramid, which has not been restored, is the Pyramid of the Old Woman, named for the mythical adoptive mother of the dwarf who built the Temple of the Magicians. The design of this pyramid is believed to be similar to that of the pyramid at Edzná, near Campeche.

The west façade of the House of the Magician, Uxmal. The left corner of the building is Temple I. The façade of Temple IV can be seen at the top of the stairway. Because of later superimpositions Temples II and III are in the interior of the pyramid. Temple V rests on the very top. Late Classic.

The unique characteristic of the architecture of the House of the Magician is the oval shape of the pyramid from the top platform down to its base. In the afternoon sun the conical shape of this massive pyramid creates some of the most interesting soft shadows to be seen in Maya architecture. There is an illusion of light and shadow sweeping around the curvilinear surface.

The Temple of the Magician, like so many other Maya structures, has superimpositions, five in all, built at various intervals of time. The first structure was Temple I, which is now partly visible at the base of the west side of the pyramid. The radiocarbon dating of a lintel inside Temple I was given as A.D. 569, a very early date for this construction at Uxmal. The second superimposition, Temple II, can be reached through a hole dug into the main stairway on the east side of the pyramid. The third and fourth superimpositions have entrances on the top west side of the pyramid. One of these entrances is in Chenes style; that is, the façade is decorated with a large mosaic-stone mask form of the rain god, Chac, whose mouth serves as the doorway. The Chenes style can be seen in some of the earlier buildings of the Late Classic Period at both Uxmal and Chichén Itzá. The style was more popularly used in the region south of the Puuc Hills; the largest of such sites there is Hochob.

The last superimposition on the House of the Magician was Temple V, built over the roof of Temple III. These additions raised the building considerably. A double stairway was then built around the Chenes façade, Temple IV, to reach Temple V. The climb on either the east or the west facing of the House of the Magician is among the steepest climbs of all Mayan ruins. The risers on the steps are especially high. The stairway on the west side of the pyramid has an angle of approximately sixty degrees. From the top platform the panoramic view of the distant landscape includes dozens of mounds yet to be investigated.

On the House of the Magician exterior decoration was kept to a minimum. On Temple V the facing is unbroken from the plaza floor to the platform except for the stairways and temple projections. On both sides of the west stairway large masks of the rain god are placed in a stepped position, one behind the other, repeating the diagonal line of the stairway. Masks were placed on stairways as early as Preclassic times on the building E-VII-sub at Uaxactún, in the Petén, and in Classic times on Structure K-5 at Piedras Negras.

A recently excavated passage running from north to south under the west stairway of the House of the Magician reveals some of the details of the early mosaic stonework on Temple I. About three hundred years probably elapsed between the construction of this building and the final superimposition.

One of the moldings on this temple is a series of shaped and

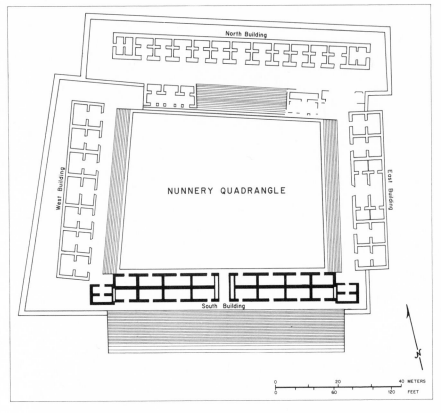

Reconstructed drawing of the Nunnery Quadrangle, Uxmal. After Marquina.

fitted stones carved in the shapes of the vertebrae of an animal. Below this molding is a row of very short spool-shaped colonettes. Below the colonettes is another molding carved in low relief with designs of frets, astronomical symbols, interlacings of vinelike decoration, fish, and human figures. Shaped "toothlike" merlons hang below this molding in a design similar to that of a wall adjoining the Portal Vault at Labná. The most beautiful single sculpture found at Uxmal is that of a head of a priest or deity with tattooed cheeks, in the jaws of a serpent. It was discovered below the doorway of the early Temple I structure, under the main stairway on the west side of the pyramid. The head has since been removed to the National Museum in Mexico City.

From the House of the Magician the next adjacent complex of buildings is that of the innovative structure called the Nunnery. This quadrangle consists of four very long buildings arranged around a central court measuring 250 by 200 feet. Each building is separate, with an open space at each corner of the quadrangle. The decorative style of each building is different, indicating a construction over a long period of time. The North Building of the Nunnery, which may be the oldest, is also the longest, approximately 270 feet. The rain-god masks that appear in great numbers on the cornice and in panels flanking the façade of the structure were a popular style in earlier buildings at Uxmal. Two other very popular decorative motifs on the frieze are undulating serpents conventionalized into geometric patterns and placed at intervals along the façade, and seated persons with bound hands, possibly prisoners, tenoned into the wall. The north wing of the quadrangle must have been the most important of the four buildings, since it faces the entrance to the quadrangle. The eleven double-vaulted chambers in the North Building, as well as the many rooms in the other three Nunnery buildings, suggest that these structures were used as a large residence. The Nunnery has seventy-four vaulted chambers in all. These buildings may have housed an institution for the training of the military, the priestly order, or the young elite, or it may have been a residence for nobles. The quadrangle courtyard was ideal for ceremonies, and the stairs to the North Building could have served as a reviewing stand. At the rear of the North Building of the Nunnery can be seen the three superimpositions of the great platform to the structure. It is obvious from the bulge in the first superimposition that the wall had been weakened by the massive masonry on top and a second retaining wall was added. At a later date a third wall was added, placed on a diagonal to create a battered wall for the platform.

The Nunnery Quadrangle, situated on a high platform, is a
unique complex at Uxmal. These buildings may have been

used as residences or as a training school. The quadrangle suggests an area for ceremonies.

The North Building of the Nunnery Quadrangle at Uxmal is the longest of the four buildings, and it may well be the oldest. Late Classic.

Detail of the intricate mosaic façade of the North Building of the Nunnery Quadrangle, Uxmal. The mosaic decoration consists of rain-god masks, stepped-fret motifs, and serpent

*forms. In the foreground is the Temple of Venus with its
unusual-shaped columns.*

Rain-god masks, one above the other, became the leitmotiv of the façade of the North Building of the Nunnery at Uxmal.

According to George Kubler, an authority on the architectural style of the Maya, the South Building is the next-oldest here. It is the entrance building to the courtyard and has a plain portal arch. From here one has an all-encompassing view of the ball court, the Palace of the Governor, and many other structures in the distance. Over the eight doors on the inside wall of the South Building are carved native-style huts, each with a rain-god mask over it. These sculptured houses are a regional art form, simplistic in conception, and exude a great amount of charm. On either side of the Portal Vault at Labná, approximately twenty miles away, native huts are also used to decorate the stone frieze. For the most part, the mosaic decoration on the façade of the South Building of the Nunnery at Uxmal is a latticework design with little embellishment compared to that of either the North or the West Building.

The East Pavilion of the Nunnery was the next structure to be built; it has decorative lines more severe than those of any other building here. Not only is the structure shorter than the others (it is only 156 feet long), but it has only five doorways, all of which face on the central court. The degree of restraint in the use of decoration is remarkable.

The fourth, or West, Building of the Nunnery was the last to be built, and it shows signs of possible Putun Maya influence in the bold and extravagant use of the serpent and the inclusion of large nude male figures tenoned into the wall of the frieze. Because of the variety of forms used, the West Building façade probably is the most interesting one to study. Over the central doorway is a throne with a feathered canopy. The figure on the throne is symbolic; it has the body of a turtle and the head of an old man. This symbolism is, no doubt, mythological or religious. It may be a later replacement by the Putun Maya of an earlier sculpture by the Puuc Maya. As in all the other buildings at the Nunnery, the façade below the medial molding is left undecorated.

Architects at Uxmal understood the principle of visual correction to the sides of building walls and compensated for it by giving the vertical walls of the Nunnery a slight negative batter, hardly noticeable to the observer. Such a refinement as this was possible only after the Puuc style had progressed for generations.

The recently restored ball court at Uxmal is in the large plaza between the Nunnery and the House of the Governor. The sidewalls are vertical and rise above very low playing benches. A short walk southwest of the ball court is the House of the Doves, so named because of the stone decorative device, similar to a dovecote, used for the roof comb. This openwork triangular motif is repeated along the entire length of the façade. The House of the Doves, constructed between A.D. 700 and 800 was built in an earlier style than that of the Nunnery and most likely was a residential palace. Although recent restoration has prevented part of the roof comb from collapsing, much more restoration work is needed here. The North Building has double-vaulted rooms, not connected, that face the north and south courts. Both façades have tumbled down, leaving intact the roof comb and segments of the

The East Building, or Pavilion, of the Nunnery Quadrangle, at Uxmal, is the smallest and stylistically the most conservative of the four structures.

The West Building of the Nunnery, Uxmal, is the richest in decoration and may well be the latest of the four structures. Late Classic.

partitions between the vaulted rooms. The portal arch of the building is very similar to that of the Nunnery.

Lintels over the doorways at Uxmal were wooden, and when they rotted, the mosaic stones above the doorways collapsed. Because of the large, consistent geometric patterns on the façades of the buildings, it was not too difficult a task for the archaeologist to determine the original pattern when reconstructing them. Since the plants in Yucatán are mostly shrubs and bushes rather than large jungle trees, the damage caused by vegetation is minor compared with the damage in the tropical area of the southern sites, where huge mahogany, ceiba, and chicle trees have crushed many buildings.

South of the House of the Doves is the Grand Pyramid, the structure most recently restored. The pyramid has nine platforms, each bearing the typical Puuc terminal molding, and an extremely wide staircase flanks the north side of the pyramid. The temple

A detail of a mosaic-stone pattern on the West Building of the Nunnery, Uxmal, shows the conventionalized design used for the background, then overlaid with a bold serpent form. Tenoned into this same wall are full figures of warriors and nude figures of men.

at the top has several unique features; among them are the great rain-god masks used liberally for decoration. Each of these masks has an unusually long sculptured projection protruding from between the eye and nose, absent from other rain-god masks. A depression on the top of the nose about an inch and a half deep may have been used for burning incense. The largest of the rain-god masks here is inside the temple; the nose, which serves as a substantial doorstep to the rear room, is eighteen inches wide. On either side of the nose are depressions that could have been used for the placement of incense or for oil and a wick to light the mask at night.

237

The House of the Doves, Uxmal, so named because of the open design resembling dovecotes that was an integral part of the

roof comb of this residential structure. The front half of the vaulted chambers has collapsed.

The corner of the temple on the Grand Pyramid, Uxmal, is decorated with rain-god masks. The tubelike stone projections between eye and nose are unusual; they also appear on a ceramic urn in the Tikal Museum depicting a deity. Below the three noses miniature sun-god heads are visible within the toothed jaws of the rain god.

Many scholars consider the House of the Turtles at Uxmal one of the most beautifully designed of the smaller structures in the Puuc Hills.

The exterior walls of the temple have several unique designs, including parrots in low relief, intricately designed molding frames, and other decorative elements. This structure was filled with rubble to provide a base for another superstructure, which was never started. For some reason the building plan must have been interrupted.

Just north of the House of the Doves is the Cemetery Group. The group is not an important one, but it encircles an intriguing small quadrangle. The small building on the west side of the courtyard has recently been restored; it is raised on a stepped platform in a style suggesting a date earlier than that of the major buildings at Uxmal. In the courtyard below this structure are four small altars or platforms. They are inscribed with hieroglyphs and symbols resembling skull-and-crossbones designs. This theme was popular among the Toltecs, and the Cemetery Group may have been

241

A detail of the list on the cornice molding on the House of the Turtles, Uxmal, where turtles are used as a harmonious decorative motif.

One of two corbeled arches separating the three sections of the Palace of the Governor, Uxmal. The doorway was closed during the later period of occupation of the site.

The Palace of the Governor at Uxmal is considered one of the most elaborate architectural structures in the Puuc Hills. Divided into three sections, this great palace is 320 feet long.

The cornice is decorated in a mosaic pattern consisting of 20,000 beautifully cut stones.

*A section of the façade on the Palace of the Governor, Uxmal. Late
Classic.*

built when the Putun Maya were infiltrating the area. Although
the name "Cemetery" seems appropriate, the area was probably
one of religious significance, used in the Terminal Classic Period
for certain rites unique to this particular court.

On the northeast corner of the plaza before the Palace of the
Governor is a small, partly restored structure, the House of the
Turtles. The building takes its place in Maya architecture as one
of the classic gems of the New World. The restraint of the architectural line, the simplicity of the decorate treatment, and the
unique handling of the cornice list have no counterpart in the
Puuc Hills. The list on the cornice of the building is decorated
with turtles, each one with a different pattern on its back. This
great platform, west of the Palace of the Governor, has been partly
excavated, revealing an earlier structure built in the Chenes-Puuc
style.

Detail of the intricate stone mosaic on the cornice of the Palace of the Governor, Uxmal. The regal headdress, still in situ, at one time adorned the head of a seated personage, now missing.

The Palace of the Governor is considered by most scholars to be architecturally the most nearly perfect building created on the grand scale in the Puuc Hills. Situated on an extremely high terrace, the structure faces east, overlooking the great plaza. At Uxmal the progressive refinement of architectural style can be appreciated by looking first at the House of the Magician, then at the Nunnery, and finally at the Palace of the Governor, the last of the extraordinary structures erected here.

The building is a massive 330-foot-long structure, resting on a five-acre platform. It has twenty-four chambers, broken by two of the highest vaulted arches created by the Maya for a palace building. At one time these arches were the doorways separating the three sections of the palace building. Later in Maya history the doorways were closed off, being filled with cut stone. The frieze above the medial molding is composed of 20,000 intricately cut and fitted pieces of mosaic stone that form a design of stepped frets, latticework, rain-god masks, and serpent motifs moving in an unbroken, flamboyant rhythm from one end of the palace to the other. The fret pattern is very old, dating back to Preclassic times, when it was used at Monte Albán. At one time sculptured figures were placed above each of the twelve doorways to the palace rooms.

As in other Puuc-style buildings, the Palace of the Governor has no decoration below the medial molding other than that on the base molding. The twenty-four rooms with vaulted ceilings suggest that the building was a palace for the families of the ruling chiefs. In the plaza in front of the palace is a two-headed jaguar throne similar to the one on the oval tablet in the Palace at Palenque. Members of the Xiu family, possibly of Putun Maya origin, occupied this building and used it as an administrative center for their conquests during Postclassic times. It was not long after this that the great ceremonial center of Uxmal was abandoned, never to be used again by the Maya.

Kabáh, Sayil, Xlapak, and Labná

During Terminal Classic times, between A.D. 850 and 900, the Maya constructed a paved *sacbé* (causeway) fifteen feet wide from Uxmal to Kabáh, a distance of approximately ten miles. Elevated causeways were common at most ceremonial centers. They can be seen at Dzibilchaltún, Chichén Itzá, and Cobá, as well as at many other sites. The longest causeway known to date stretches sixty-two miles from the site of Cobá, the largest Classic Period city in northeastern Yucatán, to Yaxuná. The causeway to Kabáh is dramatized by the presence of an extremely high undecorated arch that has been recently restored. This arch is believed to have been the gateway to the ceremonial center of Kabáh.

Kabáh is the second-largest of the Puuc Hill cities. Uxmal is by far larger and architecturally more important than Kabáh, little

The Kabáh Arch, believed to have been the gateway to the city of Kabáh. From here an elevated paved highway connected Kabáh with Uxmal.

of which has been restored. Pyramids, temple buildings, and palace-like structures dot the landscape for miles, separated by the scrub brush of this harsh, dry environment. Occasionally a deer, still hunted by the Maya for food, is seen in these thickets.

The Palace of the Masks (called by the Maya Codz Poop) is the most elaborately decorated of the visible buildings of Kabáh. It is reminiscent of Chenes-style architecture and is 151 feet long. The façade of this palacelike structure is completely covered with 250 rain-god masks, each made of thirty units of mosaic stone. The carving on the repeated mask forms is extremely deep. Shadows cast by the play of sunlight around the mosaic forms soften the harshness of the stone and make the repetition of form less monotonous. The decoration covers the façade both above and below the medial molding, and one row of masks extends below the base

The Palace of the Masks, Kabáh, is executed in the Chenes style. The façade is completely covered with rain-god masks

that extend from the terminal molding to the structure's platform. Late Classic.

A detail of the Palace of the Masks, at Kabáh. The intricately fitted mosaic stones create an unusual play of light in the late-afternoon sun.

molding. The nose of one rain-god mask, like that on the mask in the Great Pyramid at Uxmal, is used as a step to the five doorways—a decided overuse of the mask form. If the two cuplike depressions on either side of the nose of every mask were used for burning incense or an oil wick, the gallery of masks must have created quite a dramatic scene when all the burners were alight. The Palace of the Masks has ten chambers; each of the five doorways leads into a double-roomed apartment. The building was crowned by an open roof comb, the remains of which can be seen today. To watch the sunset turn the façade of the Palace of the Masks to burnished gold is an experience long to be remembered.

A footpath east of the temple leads to two other large, palace-like structures, El Palacio and Las Columnas. Unlike the Palace of the Masks, they have rather plain façades. The façade of El Palacio is distinct from that of the other palaces because of the very wide

The Palace of Sayil, one of the finest of the larger structures in the Puuc Hills. The building contains more than one hundred rooms and rises on three terraced platforms. Late Classic.

cornice, modified to lean slightly inward and thus create a mansardlike roof. El Palacio has two stories and a high, open roof comb. There are seven doorways in the façade; two of the wider doorways are supported in the center by a rounded column that holds the weight of the lintel. Las Columnas, just a little farther on the path behind El Palacio, is in partial ruin. Much of the mosaic stone has fallen to the ground or has been removed for construction, a process which has gone on ever since the time of the Spanish conquest. Enough remains, however, to indicate the general decoration of the façade. For the most part, banded colonettes and shaped-stone spools were used to decorate both these buildings. On Las Columnas much longer colonettes were added below the medial molding on either side of each doorway. The doors here have a slightly trapezoidal shape, the top being slightly narrower

253

The second floor of the Palace at Sayil was designed with porticoed chambers. The circular columns bulge slightly in the center. Colonettes play an important part in the design of the façade.

than the bottom. Other structures at Kabáh have the same kind of door.

At one time the most difficult, hard-riding, dust-eating Jeep trip one could take through any backcountry bush was the trip to Sayil, Xlapak, and Labná. In the rainy season the water holes and the flies were numerous beyond belief. Today, however, a new road has been opened, and these very impressive Maya ruins can be reached in comfort by bus or car.

The Sayil archaeological zone is extensive, but most of it still lies under the dense acacia trees, bushes, and vines that converted this dry limestone country into a jungle. Although pottery dating back to Preclassic times has been discovered, all the structures visible today date from the Late Classic Period. The Palace of Sayil is another extraordinary masterpiece of Maya architecture.

The cornice above the doorway of the second story of the Palace at Sayil is decorated with a "diving god" and mythological creatures in carved stone. This building, like the others in the Puuc Hills, is made of limestone. Late Classic.

Its length, 236 feet, is approximately two-thirds the length of the Palace of the Governor at Uxmal. Restoration of various parts of this palace in recent years has revealed the true beauty of line, the delicate balance and restraint of decoration, and the flair with which the architects handled open galleries, patios, and columned porticoes. The unusual orange coloring of the limestone exterior is no more than a surface stain. The soil that had covered the ruins here for many centuries contained iron oxide that stained the stone.

The Sayil Palace has three recessed stories containing fifty double chambers. It is approached by a wide stairway that extends from ground level to the third floor. On close examination the building is not symmetrical; part of the first floor was built at an earlier date, and when the palace was enlarged, the old building was incorporated into the total design. The façades of the first and third floors are restrained in decoration, but the architects were lavish in their plan for the second floor. Here round columns were used for the porticoes of the eight apartments, opening the rooms onto the deck of the first floor and allowing much light to penetrate them. These rounded columns are unusual in that they were carved with a slight bulge. Square capitals hold up the stone lintels of the doorways. The walls between the columns consist of double rows of colonettes. Above the medial molding is a frieze of rounded, spindle colonettes, a gigantic rain-god mask with exposed teeth over the central façade, and diving gods flanked by creatures resembling small serpents or fish. The diving gods reappeared five hundred years later in Maya history in a degenerate style at Tulúm, a little site overlooking the Caribbean.

The Palace of Sayil was crowned by an openwork roof comb of considerable height. A view of the surrounding country is spectacular from the rooftop of this palace: old Maya buildings can be seen projecting above the dry brush of the countryside, and the Puuc Hills form an undulating line on the horizon.

A room on the north end of the palace is unusual in having a porticoed inner chamber with two columns. Porticoed rooms on this and other structures in the Puuc area were generally placed on the doorways of the outer walls of the buildings. Just behind the Palace is a large circular stone catch basin, about thirty feet across, for collecting rainwater that flowed into a cistern. A very short distance from the Sayil Palace is a temple structure on a small pyramid called El Mirador. The remains of a *sacbé* connect the two structures. El Mirador is in poor repair, but its high roof comb is still intact, silhouetted against the jungle brush. A short walk on a footpath from El Mirador leads to a sculpture of a nude male with enlarged genitals. The sculpture may have been used for some kind of fertility rite and is believed to be a cult figure from Postclassic times, possibly used by the Putun Maya.

En route to Labná is the small archaeological zone of Xlapak, meaning Old Walls. For many years it was completely covered by the jungle except for one corner of a small building that may have been a residential structure. Recently it has been partly restored and the surrounding area cleared of brush. The style of the architecture is reserved. In typical Puuc tradition the lower zone of the façade is left plain. The frieze above the medial molding is composed of a fret pattern and large rain-god masks extending to the corners of the building. On the corners of the structure are engaged columns, unique to the Puuc Hills and surrounding territory. Similarly rounded columns can be seen on the House of the Three Lintels at Old Chichén (the architectural style at Old Chichén reveals much influence from the Puuc Hills region). Another comparable type of engaged column is used on the corner of the Labná Palace and on three of the corners of the Labná Vault.

The Palace at Labná, 276 feet long and one of the largest of its kind in the Puuc area, is similar in style to the Palace at Sayil. Its construction probably began at an earlier date than that of the latter, and it went through many structural changes over a long period of years. Parts of the palace were never finished. If this palace is ever completely restored, some of the grandeur will be apparent. The cistern built into the second floor to catch rainwater still holds water today. On the second story of the palace is an arrangement of apartments. The porticoes are similar to those on the Sayil Palace, with rounded columns in the middle of doorways to support the lintels.

There are many attractive panels and other kinds of decoration on the Palace at Labná. One of the finest Maya carvings of a serpent's head, with jaws fully open and holding a sculptured human head, is on the east corner of the façade. Just below this serpent are three engaged, rounded columns. This building is the only one known to have three columns serving as the corner of the building's exterior. Others, however, may be excavated at some future time.

A rain-god mask on the adjacent wall of the palace is in excellent condition and is one of the largest of its type. Tenoned human figures were inserted into the frieze of the cornice on either side of this large mask. Naturalistic sculptural forms were used on the Nunnery at Uxmal and at Labná, and there are indications of such forms on the flying façade of the Castillo. Abstract and

At Xlapak this restored building, possibly a residence, is designed in the Puuc style, in which the façade below the medial

molding is left plain. Rain-god masks and a stepped-fret pat-
tern decorate the cornice. Late Classic.

The Palace at Labná is an unusually long structure, built over many centuries but never finished. The cornice of the Palace

and some panels on the façade are decorated in mosaic stone. Late Classic.

The Labná Palace has three stories. On the second story a porticoed chamber overlooks the great plaza in front of the Palace. A water cistern, or chultun, was an integral part of the design for the second floor. Chultunes of this type hold about 7,500 gallons of water.

geometric motifs, however, were preferred. Where naturalistic forms were used, they were confined to tenoned figures placed above the medial molding on the frieze or on the roof comb.

The Castillo is a pyramid-temple structure just southwest of the palace. Although some restoration has been carried out on the temple of the Castillo, the pyramidal base has yet to be reconstructed.

A recently restored structure, the East Building, is just east of the Palace. It may have been a residential structure for one of the elite. The East Building is typical of the Puuc style, in which colonettes are used above the medial molding and the lower part of the structure is plain.

Adjacent to the Castillo is the most noted and finest of all

A corner of the cornice of the Palace at Labná has an intricately carved serpent whose open mouth contains a human head. Late Classic.

portal arches in the Maya area, the Labná Vault. The vault was intended as a passageway from one courtyard to another. It would seem that the western court was the most important, because the arch has a lavish mosaic frieze on that side, whereas the mosaic frieze on the east side was designed in a simplified geometric pattern. The skillfully executed and fitted pattern on the west side of the arch is a triumph of mosaic-stone design. Two doorways lead into small rooms within the arch. The frieze on both sides of the vault is decorated with stylized thatched huts, representing a type of house still used in Yucatán today. This important portal vault, like many other buildings in the Puuc Hills, was topped by an openwork roof comb. The roof comb here is a stepped, openwork triangle. Roof combs in this area never took on the importance they

263

Over one of the doors of the Palace at Labná is one of the largest rain-god masks ever created by the Maya. Late Classic.

attained in the Petén or Usumacinta regions, where they dominated the temples.

Sparsely populated today, the Puuc Hills maintained a population of around 22,500 during Classic times, according to estimates projected by Sylvanus G. Morley. The chultunes, artificial wells for the storage of rainwater, were controlling factors in population density. Later, after the Spaniards arrived, populations were decimated by diseases that were previously unknown to the Maya and for which they lacked resistance. Measles was responsible for the deaths of over half of the people in Honduras alone. Smallpox, influenza, malaria, and dysentery also took very heavy tolls. In some areas up to 90 percent of the Maya population was wiped out. The Maya living in the Puuc Hills today are descendants of the few survivors. Their life pattern has changed little from that of their ancestors over the past thousand years.

Little of the Castillo at Labná has been restored. The base pyramid is still a heap of rubble. A flying façade increases the height of this templelike structure.

Adjacent to the Castillo is the famed Labná Vault. On each side of the arch is a small room, and on the cornice are two miniature houses executed in mosaic stone. The openwork roof comb is partly intact. Late Classic.

Edzna

Driving through the interesting old colonial city of Campeche, catching vistas of the blue-green sea through arches of old fortified walls, one is tempted to linger here for a few days. Just thirty miles southeast of Campeche, in a flat savannah country sprinkled with farms and studded with water holes, is a very impressive ancient Maya city seen by few tourists. Edzna has now been partly excavated to reveal a large Late Classic city with a ceremonial center composed of impressive pyramid temples, palaces, and other majestic structures. Because of its location Edzna must have been an important urban center; the overland trade route between the Gulf Coast and the Puuc, Río Bec, and Chenes areas and the route from the coast to the Southern Lowlands formed a crossroads at Edzna. Cultural ties both at Edzna and at Cobá reflect the commercial network with the central Petén. Both cities probably had depots for such marketable goods as cotton and salt that could readily be transported on overland routes to Hochob, Becan, and Río Bec and from those cities to the central Petén. Becan is known to have been fortified with a moat and ramps in Early Classic times, and its vigorous building program in Late Classic suggests the commercial importance of the city.

Excavation at Edzna was started in 1958 under the leadership of George F. Andrews and has continued periodically since that time. Reconstruction of the major pyramid was a tremendous task, and other structures around it have been restored as well, but most of Edzna is still covered by underbrush.

The ceremonial plazas at Edzna are spacious, and, judging from the plan of the city, they must have been ideally suited for ceremonial life. The structures and platforms surrounding the plazas could have been used for administrative, religious, or residential purposes. Besides the major ceremonial area there are seventeen additional complexes as far as two miles from the center of the city. The architectural style of Edzna reflects the beginnings of the Puuc style popularly developed in the Late Classic cities in northern Yucatán. Although the structures visible today of Edzna are Late Classic, the area may well have been populated in Early Classic

Templo Major (Structure 19), Edzna. The pyramid has a series of rooms on each of the major platforms, an unusual feature. The pyramid is crowned with a temple. Late Classic.

times, and further excavation may reveal structures from that period. Under the present pyramid is a smaller pyramid temple that must be of an earlier date. There is also indication of Preclassic occupation at Edzna. As seen today, the many structures are all adjacent to *bajos,* small depressions in which water accumulates. This may well be the reason the city was founded in this particular region, for the wetlands would be ideal for raised fields and double crops. In addition, there is evidence of canals, important for drainage in this method of agriculture.

The Main Acropolis at Edzna stands on a platform 22 feet above ground level. On the west side is the Templo Major (Structure 19), a five-story pyramid-temple structure reaching a height of 126 feet. The four stories of rooms, visible on the west side and forming the pyramid proper, are unique. These importantly placed rooms may have been used by the rulers as a residential area or

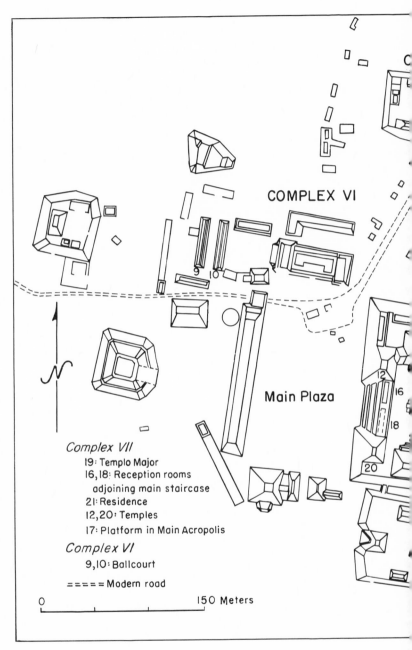

COMPLEX VI

Main Plaza

Complex VII
19: Templo Major
16,18: Reception rooms
adjoining main staircase
21: Residence
12,20: Temples
17: Platform in Main Acropolis

Complex VI
9,10: Ballcourt

===== Modern road

0   150 Meters

Edzna. After Andrews.

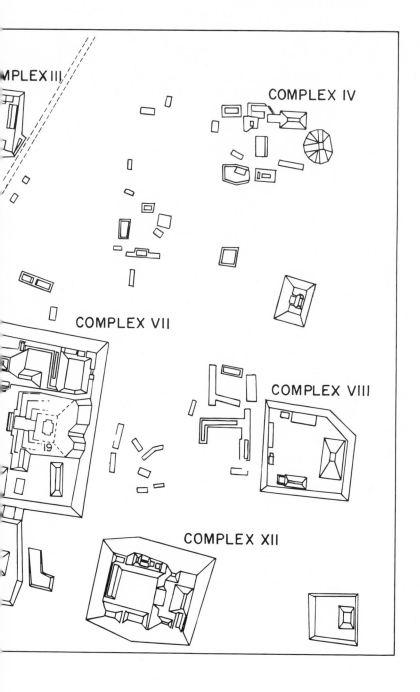

COMPLEX III

COMPLEX IV

COMPLEX VII

COMPLEX VIII

19

COMPLEX XII

Structures 21 (in the foreground) and 20 (in the distance) form part of the restored section of Edzna. Late Classic.

by priests in connection with religious ceremonies in the temple on the summit. The first and second platforms to the pyramid have passageways under the main stairway, so that persons could easily pass the horizontal length of the façade without crossing the stairway. Three steps on the stairway from the platform to the pyramid are carved with glyphs and are in a good state of preservation. At the very top of this pyramid is a temple that differs from other Maya temples in having exterior doorways on both the east and the west sides. The doorway on the east side of the temple leads to a single room sealed off from the other rooms in the building. This room may have been a later addition to the temple. On the west side the great staircase leads to three doorways with four interconnecting rooms. It appears that the interior of the temple was altered over a period of time. The roof comb is twenty feet high, designed with vertical strips of stone masonry, and there is evidence of tenoned sculptures on the facing. This kind of roof comb has similarities with roof combs on the small temple structures at Palenque as well as those in the Puuc Hills area.

On the south side of the main plaza is an unusually long,

raised pyramidal substructure with an administrative or palace building on the top platform (Structure 21). This interesting building which had a thatch roof during its occupancy, has been restored. Since excavations at Edzna reveal few indications of masonry roofs, timber-and-thatch roofs must have been in common use for masonry structures at this time. The four stepped platforms in front of the main stairway to Structure 21 are unusually large and may have been used as an outdoor reception area for the elite. East of Structure 21 is the partly restored Structure 23, a much smaller building on a high platform. Immediately west of Structure 21 is Structure 20, which has also been partly restored, and from the top platform there is a beautiful view of the Templo Major in the late-afternoon light. Adjacent to Structure 20 are two long, narrow buildings (Structures 16 and 18), possibly used for receptions, separated by a narrow entrance leading into the Main Plaza. The center of the plaza has a low platform (Structure 17) that is large enough to have been used for plays, music recitals, or rituals connected with the ceremonial center.

The north side of the Main Plaza has another series of palace-like structures with courtyards that complete the enclosure of this acropolis. West of the great ceremonial complex is another group of structures that have been partly excavated. In this area is a ball court (Structures 9 and 10) that has not been restored. Other complexes reach into the distance as far as the eye can see, but none of them has been excavated or restored to any extent. A large number of sculptured monuments (Ruz, 1970, reports nineteen stelae) were erected at Edzna, but some of them have been removed to the museum in Campeche. Those remaining at the site are badly eroded by the weather, and some are broken. According to deciphered glyphs, the carvings were executed from A.D. 633 to 810, in Late Classic times.

The many complexes at Edzna are spatially oriented to the Main Acropolis. The dominance of the major pyramid temple emphasizes this relationship. In the afternoon light this vast abandoned city casts mauve shadows on the grasses and brush and into the wet *bajos* that have helped sustain life here over the centuries. This Maya city, once visited, can never be forgotten.

9   Northern Yucatán: Chichén Itzá

Heading north from the tropical rain forests of the Petén, leaving behind the great stands of mahogany, cedar, sapodilla, and other hardwoods, one enters Yucatán, where the landscape changes abruptly. The Yucatán Peninsula is a dry coastal tableland covered with a thick undergrowth of plants that are able to survive with little rain and in shallow soil. Surface water and streams are practically nonexistent because of the porous limestone base.

The present-day Maya homes along the road are constructed in the same way as were Maya dwellings in Preclassic times. The oval houses are built with a framework of slender tree branches ingeniously lashed together to withstand the hurricanes that blow in from the coast. The sides of the houses are woven of twigs. Red clay mixed with straw or grass is thickly plastered on the sidewalls and whitewashed. A thatch roof of palm fronds completes the usual rural house. Television antennas projecting above the thatch roofs are not unusual. These houses are relatively cool because of the height of the open ceilings and the adobe sides. Hammocks are used for sleeping. Since the water table is only about twenty-five feet below the surface, most houses have wells. A small shed in the backyard is used for cooking. Although men are likely to wear typical Western dress for work today, Maya women are usually seen wearing heavily embroidered huipils.

For many centuries Yucatán has prospered from its sisal industry. Plants of the genus *Agave*, used for sisal, can be seen growing along the road for miles into the distance. Occasionally large mounds, sites of ancient ruins, break the horizon. Some of the limestone caves in this area have been occupied from time to time; a Late Preclassic relief carving in Loltún Cave depicts a full figure that shows the stylistic influence of early Maya and Izapan art. One of the larger ruins seen en route to Chichén Itzá (which means Mouth of the Well of the Itzá) is in the little village of Izamal.

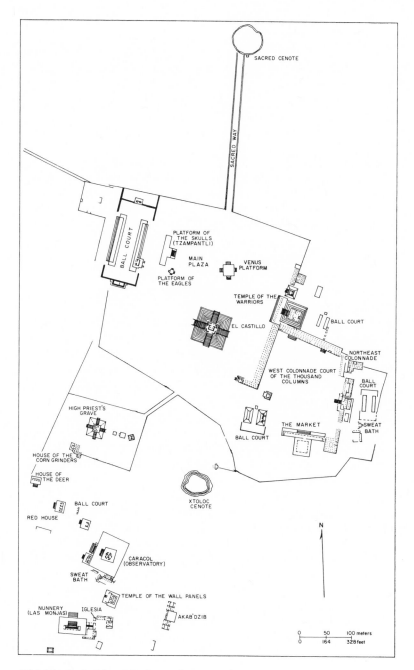

Chichén Itzá. After Morley and Brainerd.

This site, along with Acancéh and Dzibilchaltún, was very active from Preclassic through Early Classic times. The influence of Teotihuacán can be seen in the use of a *talud-tablero*, the dominant architectural form on each side of the pyramid (the *talud* is the sloping base; the *tablero*, the vertical paneled plane above the *talud*). The stucco decoration here is reminiscent of that on the Early Classic buildings in the North Acropolis at Tikal, and Acancéh has a similar stucco decoration. All of these Yucatán sites are only a short drive from Mérida. Yucatán has been continuously occupied since the early history of man in the Western Hemisphere. Hunting and fishing bands had infiltrated the peninsula by 8,000 B.C.

The Early Classic Period (A.D. 300-600) saw the continual growth of Maya settlements, and by Late Classic times (600-900) the Maya had established a large city at Chichén Itzá. The architecture was in a style similar to that of cities in the Puuc Hills. Chichén Itzá and Cobá were the two largest cities in the northern area of the Yucatán Peninsula. Their location gave them control of the trade routes, both by water and by land, from the Caribbean to the Gulf of Mexico. Important produce such as cotton, salt, fish, and shells could be traded to the inland cities farther south. Today at Chichén Itzá we can see the few remaining Maya structures from this Late Classic Period. The Nunnery, the Red House, the House of the Deer, the Iglesia, Akab Dzib, and most of the buildings in Old Chichén were part of the city at that time. The city is believed to have been abandoned at the end of the Late Classic Period.

It should be pointed out that the Spanish or Spanish-derived names of buildings, such as Castillo, Nunnery, Caracol, and Iglesia, have nothing to do with their original functions. The conquistadors merely named them for similar-appearing types of buildings in Spain. The Maya structures had been abandoned several centuries before the arrival of Cortés and his army, and their functions were unknown to the Spaniards.

As we have noted, in Terminal Classic times (A.D. 800-1000) migrant groups, possibly Putun Maya (also called Chontal), infiltrated the Maya area. The Putun Maya were composed of several large, independent groups ruled by dynastic families, united by a common language, and occupying the lowland territories of Tabasco and Campeche from the Grijalva to the Champotón rivers during Terminal and Postclassic times. They were aggressive warriors, merchants, and expansionists who apparently monopolized the crucial seacoast trade routes around the Yucatán Peninsula and the riverine trade along the Gulf. Joseph Ball and J. Eric Thompson say that Itzá was the name of one of the Putun Maya groups who were to occupy Chichén Itzá and may also have been the intrusive group that settled in Seibal in Terminal Classic times. Similarities in relief carvings, such as the limestone panels on the Tzompantli at Chichén Itzá and Stela 13 at Seibal, are readily noticed. The culture of the Putun Maya expresses many characteristics associated with people of central Mexico and the Gulf Coast. The Toltec culture is strongly reflected in their arts, and it is quite possible that the Putun were politically allied with the Toltec as well as with other peoples in the Valley of Mexico.

According to legend, a large contingent of the Toltec ruling class and their warriors left Tula, their homeland in the highlands of Mexico, and migrated to Yucatán. They supposedly established their capital at Chichén Itzá, the old Maya city, and utilized it for their own purposes. The legend, widely quoted in literature, telling of Quetzalcoatl leaving his homeland with a band of warriors and migrating south, is hardly sufficient evidence to determine who settled at Chichén Itzá and when that settlement occurred. It is possible that Chichén Itzá was settled by the Putun Maya before the Toltec city of Tula was constructed.

The Toltec were an aggressive warrior tribe who migrated from the north into the Valley of Mexico and other areas in the south. Their culture was an eclectic one gleaned from Teotihuacán and the Veracruz area. They established a capital at Tula, and Chichén Itzá may have been another of their allied cities. Thus Chichén Itzá, the old Maya city, is a mixture of both Mexican and Maya architectural styles. The Maya structures, however, date from a much earlier period.

Another area in Yucatán that felt the influence of a non-Maya culture was Uxmal, as is evident in the Nunnery and the Cemetery

Group stone carvings. If they were not Toltec, these arrivals may have been members of one of the several independent Mexicanized Putun Maya groups itinerant in Terminal Classic times and even earlier. If they were Putun Maya, they could have been allied with the Toltec in the management and control of trade routes. Although the relationship of Chichén Itzá with Tula is unclear, there must have been close commercial ties.

Murals at Cacaxtla, in the state of Puebla, indicate the presence of Maya in that area, and at Xochicalco the sculptures on the Pyramid of the Plumed Serpent depict the Maya, in typical Maya clothing, seated as great lords. This kind of evidence supports the theory that the Putun Maya were in some kind of alliance with several northern areas to secure or manage the trade network (Robert J. Sharer) at a time when Mexico was in a state of transition. The Classic Mexican cities Teotihuacán, Monte Albán, and Cholula were in cultural decline or abandoned by Terminal Classic times, and the militant Postclassic Toltec were the next to ascend to power in this area, followed by the Aztec in Late Postclassic.

The Itzá Maya were a Putun Maya group, and it may have been those peoples who took over Chichén Itzá in the Terminal Classic Period. There is also accumulating evidence that it was a Putun Maya group from Northern Yucatán who invaded the Pasión River region and established itself at Seibal. According to Arthur Miller, one of the battle scenes in the Temple of the Jaguar (Temple A) at Chichén Itzá documents this invasion.

Fragmentary data indicate that Chichén Itzá could be earlier than Tula, the Toltec capital in Mexico. For example, the architectural style at Tula seems provincial compared with the fine style of architecture at Chichén Itzá. More investigation will be needed before any conclusions can be reached on this chronology.

The early period of construction at Chichén Itzá in Late Classic times is in the Puuc Maya style. For the most part the Mexicanized invaders spared the older Classic Maya buildings but altered other structures to suit their needs and tastes. The Mexicanized Maya ruled at Chichén Itzá for two centuries before the area was again abandoned in the early part of the thirteenth century. Their political control of this area in Terminal Classic days and their mana-

The Castillo, rising 79 feet above the Main Plaza, is the highest struc-
ture at Chichén Itzá. The stairway faces the path leading to the Well
of Sacrifice. Inside this pyramid is a smaller one, constructed at an
earlier time.

gerial control of seagoing trade routes coincide with the cultural
decline of the Maya in the Southern Lowlands. Some evidence of
this is the large quantity of Fine Orange pottery from the Gulf
Coast, probably brought by sea trade, found at Chichén Itzá. This
pottery was later mass-produced by the Yucatán Maya.

The distance from Mérida to Chichén Itzá is only seventy-
five miles. Looming on the horizon as one approaches the archaeological zone is the tallest temple here, the Castillo, gleaming in
the golden sunlight. Standing on a north-south axis, this pyramid is
constructed of nine platforms and has a central stairway on each
of the four sides. Each platform diminishes in size from bottom to
top, creating the illusion of a much taller pyramid. The Castillo
is seventy-nine feet high, approximately one-third the height of

Temple IV at Tikal. On the top platform is a temple with a doorway facing each of the stairs, but the main portico faces north. From here the priests could view the spacious plaza and watch processionals to the Sacred Cenote—the famed Well of Sacrifice—a short distance north.

On purpose, only two sides of the Castillo have been restored, enabling scholars and other visitors to see on the other two sides the condition of the pyramid before archaeological work began. The Castillo has many characteristics typically Toltec in style, such as the merlons on the roof that form a crest similar to the crests on the serpent wall at Tula, serpent columns, and warriors carved in relief on the doorjambs and columns of the portico. Within this pyramid is an earlier one that probably dates from the beginning of Mexicanized Maya occupancy of the area. The climb up the inner stairway, beneath the present north stairway, to the temple of this inner building will be one of great expectation, for it is here that the marvelous red jaguar throne, studded with jade encrustations, can be seen. A fine chacmool, a sculpture of a reclining figure, stands at the entrance to this temple.

The archaeological zone of Chichén Itzá covers approximately four square miles. At one time it was occupied by the famous Itzá family, who later returned to Flores, at Lake Petén, and there held out against the Spaniards until the seventeenth century.

At the turn of the century Edward Thompson, an American, bought the hacienda at Chichén Itzá for five hundred dollars and carried out archaeological excavations. His most daring adventure was the dredging of the famed cenote to retrieve its treasures. Some of the pieces recovered were priceless artifacts of previous centuries. A jade bead from Palenque found in the cenote is dated A.D. 690, and another jade bead, possibly from Piedras Negras, is dated 706. Gold circular disks thrown into the cenote were purposely crumbled if plain, and if decorated were ceremonially torn into pieces. The embossed and engraved designs on the gold plaques are especially fine in execution, but they can be appreciated today only by seeing an artist's rendering of what they looked like before their destruction. The subject usually is one of a "Toltec" warrior subjecting or in combat with the Maya. Gold was not introduced into Mesoamerica until Postclassic times, after the tenth century. Gold pieces in the cenote were imported items from Panama or Costa Rica. The copper objects, especially the large quantities of bells, may have been imported from the Oaxaca area or from some other part of Mexico. Because the Yucatán Peninsula is a limestone platform, no minerals of this type are found there. The lime water helped preserve the copper objects in the well. The Peabody Museum has most of the collection from the cenote. The rest is in the National Museum of Anthropology and History, in Mexico City, and a large collection of cenote jades are in the museum in Mérida.

Between 1923 and 1943 the Carnegie Institution financed extensive excavations and restorations at Chichén Itzá, directed by Sylvanus G. Morley. Only a few of the buildings have been restored, however. The rest remain, by the hundreds, in great mounds covered by vegetation of the bush country.

At Chichén Itzá nine ball courts are known, but only one has been restored. There is no other ball court in Mesoamerica as impressive for its size or as well integrated with the temples and other tectonic forms of the ball-court area as this restored court at Chichén Itzá. It is one of the great architectural marvels built by the original inhabitants of the New World. Not only is it the largest court (545 feet long), but it has unusually high vertical sides. The court's vertical walls rise to a splendid height and are interrupted by the large, delicately carved circular rings placed in the center of each wall, through which the ball had to pass. The rings are twenty feet above the playing ground.

On the two slanting walls, called benches, running the length of either side of the ball court, are six sculptured reliefs, each forty feet long, placed in panels at three intervals. Virtually the same scene is depicted on all the panels: a victorious ball team holds the severed head of a member of the losing team. A design of seven snake heads represents the blood issuing from the neck. Carved green vegetation also extends from the severed neck and covers a large part of the relief. This stylistic idea probably was an influence from the Classic Veracruz area. The ball court bas-relief at Chichén Itzá offers some information about the nature of

Chichén Itzá boasts the largest ball court in the Americas. It is a splendid structure 545 feet long and 223 feet wide. On its upper platform is the Temple of the Jaguar. The second-

*largest ball court excavated so far in Mesoamerica is in Tula;
it is 380 feet long.*

the game, the number of players on the teams, the clothing worn by the players, and the final ceremony. The relief carving on the northeast panel of the ball court is considered to be the most skillfully executed.

At either end of the ball court is a small temple. The north temple is decorated with frescoes which can be seen under the portico of the façade. The south building may have been used as a reviewing stand for the elite members of the society rather than as a temple building.

The most imposing of the three buildings facing the ball court is the Temple of the Jaguars (Temple A). The second story of this building is reached by an extremely steep stairway at the east end of the court. The balustrade is carved to represent a plumed serpent. The Temple of the Jaguars bears several similarities to the main temple at Tula. There are the serpent columns, very beautifully carved, that support the lintels of the very wide doorway. The doorjambs, like those at Tula, are executed with the usual Toltec warrior themes. The frieze above the medial molding, composed of a repeated jaguar and circular shield motif executed in a flat relief, is very similar to the jaguar frieze on the Tula pyramid. A battered wall is at the base of the temple building, an element typical of Postclassic structures of Toltec and Aztec design.

Within the chamber of the Temple of the Jaguars is one of the few murals extant in the southern area of Mesoamerica. It has been badly defaced; however, enough remains to see that the main theme is a battle scene with hundreds of warriors laying siege to a Maya village.

The first floor of the Temple of the Jaguars faces the Main Plaza and was constructed earlier than the top temple, possibly at the same time that the inner temple of the Castillo was built. The structure has an open portico supported by two square columns. The columns and the porticoed chamber are decorated in low-relief carvings.

The Tzompantli is a low-lying platform just east of the ball court. The carved reliefs on the vertical walls of the platform represent four different subjects. Most of the platform has reliefs of a skull rack and here some of the original paint has been preserved.

The Tzompantli, adjacent to the ball court at Chichén Itzá, has some fine relief carvings on the vertical sides. Known as a "skull-rack" design, the carving shows skulls on poles. The original paint is clearly visible.

On another section of the platform are relief sculptures depicting a sacrificial scene very similar to the one depicted on the benches of the ball court. A third section of this structure has panels in low relief showing eagles eating human hearts. These alternate with panels showing a warrior with shield and arrows. His rib cage and bones of the legs and arms show the skeletal structure, and many snake heads are shown coming from behind and extending from the sides of the warrior. From his skeletal form and his attire he may represent a deified warrior. At Seibal, in Guatemala, Stela 13 is decorated in a similar manner, with a snake entwined around the waist of a ruler and six snakes projecting

283

One of the many stone panels on the Tzompantli, Chichén Itzá, showing a warrior with several serpents extending from his sides. His legs are skeletal, possibly indicating that he is a warrior in the guise of a deity. He holds three arrows in his left hand and a shield on his right arm. Postclassic.

The two platforms known as the Platform of the Jaguars and Eagles and the Platform of Venus are in the Main Plaza at Chichén Itzá. They may have been used for dances, oratory, or music. A decoration on the façade shows an eagle eating a human heart, a popular theme here and at Tula.

from his skirt. A scroll issues from the man's mouth. The dress and the style of the relief carving suggest that the two sculptured monuments result from cultural contact between these two far-flung areas. The infiltrating Mexicanized Maya did eventually bring with them political control. This evidence suggests that parts of Chichén Itzá and Seibal are Terminal Classic in period.

Since the bas-reliefs on the Tzompantli at Chichén Itzá were associated with human sacrifice, it was expected that excavations here would reveal skeletal remains, but none have been found. In areas of intense humidity combined with a high level of acidity skeletal forms disintegrate. This is not likely, however, in such a dry area as the limestone country of the Yucatán Peninsula.

A short distance from the Main Plaza at Chichén Itzá is the Sacred Cenote, often called the Well of Sacrifice. This cenote has proved to be a treasure-house of artifacts, items cast into it over several centuries. On the opposite edge of the well can be seen the ruins of the Temple of Xtoloc.

Ceremonial platforms were popular at Chichén Itzá, as well as at Tula and Tenochtitlán, in Postclassic times. Two platforms at Chichén Itzá are nearly alike, both having stairs on all four sides of the structures, balustrades of feathered serpents, and reliefs in panels on the friezes. On the Platform of the Jaguar and Eagles the frieze shows these creatures eating human hearts. Both animals represent fraternal military societies popular among the Toltec and Aztec in Postclassic times. A platform like this one may have functioned as a reviewing stand for the military, as a stage for dancers or musicians, or as a place from which to announce the proclamations of the chiefs or ruler. On a cornice molding above the frieze on the Venus Platform is a delicate low relief in which a fish swims in a water-wave motif. The dominant frieze on this platform, however, has very large plaques depicting an open-jawed serpent from whose mouth a human head projects—supposedly one of the symbols for the planet Venus. Other symbols here may also relate to the planet.

A short walk north from the Main Plaza leads to the legendary cenote, the Well of Sacrifice. Very early in the morning, when the air is cool, the beautiful motmot and other tropical birds can be seen gliding through the air around this ceremonial well. The cenote is large, covering a surface area of nearly an acre. Evidently the well was used exclusively for ritual purposes over a long period of time, perhaps as long as five hundred years. At the edge of the cenote are the remains of a small stone structure called the Temple of Xtoloc. It may have been used for ritual purposes during sacrificial ceremonies here. The remains of skeletons retrieved from the well prove that the persons sacrificed were not all virgin girls but adult men and women as well as children. From a narrow path around the edge of the cenote is a picturesque view of the well and the pathway leading to the Castillo, rising above the horizon in the distance.

The Temple of the Warriors, adjacent to the Castillo, is an impressive building similar to the Pyramid of Quetzalcóatl at Tula. The structure at Chichén Itzá, however, is much larger, more finely decorated, and more complex than that at Tula.

The Temple of the Warriors rises in four platforms and is

The Temple of the Warriors at Chichén Itzá is "Toltec" in design. At the northern Toltec capital, Tula, is a structure similar to this one but poorly executed in comparison. Postclassic.

flanked on the west and south sides by approximately two hundred round and square columns. The square columns are carved in low relief, repeating a warrior theme. In a few places the original paint is still visible on the columns. They are not monolithic but were cemented together in sections, given a very thin coating of plaster, and then painted in brilliant colors.

The Temple of the Warriors is approached by a broad stairway with a plain, stepped ramp on either side. These ramps are surmounted with figures of standard-bearers designed to hold flags. As far as is known, sculptured standard-bearers were not used by the Classic Maya. They were used, however, by both the Aztec and the Toltec at their respective capitals. Serpent columns carved on a monumental scale were used to hold the wooden lintels, long since disintegrated, above the doorways. Decorative feathers on the head of the serpent and astronomical signs over the eyes are finely carved in the limestone. On the top of each head is a shallow basin that may have been used for an oil-and-wick lamp at night. On this same structure each rain-god mask has a cuplike basin above the nose, possibly for the same purpose. The lights would have created quite a spectacle for ceremonial occasions.

The façade of the Temple of the Warriors is plain, broken by an occasional panel of rain-god masks or a serpent holding a human head in its open jaws. The wood-and-stucco roof perished centuries ago.

Beneath this temple is a much earlier one, perhaps one of the first constructions in Terminal Classic times. The importance of the inner structure is the well-preserved original color of the stone columns. The walls were painted with murals. Fortunately they were sketched and photographed before they began to disintegrate from exposure to air when the temple was first opened.

Several sculptured chacmools have been found at Chichén Itzá. There is a fine one in the inner temple of the Castillo, and another at the top of the stairway to the Temple of the Warriors. This kind of sculpture, of a man seated and leaning back in a rather uncomfortable position on his elbows, is also known in other regions of Mesoamerica. Nevertheless, the sculptors at Chichén Itzá defined a specific style for the chacmool and used this sculptural form in many of the buildings. This monument may have been used as a place to leave offerings for religious ceremonies or as an oil basin for a ceremonial fire. Centuries later the Aztec continued to use the chacmool sculptures in their ceremonial cities in the Mexican highlands.

On the south side of the Temple of the Warriors are two friezes in the *tableros* that run the length of the sidewall. These skillfully executed reliefs depict bears, jaguars, and eagles. Interspersed with the animals is a male human figure, possibly representing a deity, who seems to be floating on his back. In his arms is a ceremonial object that looks like some kind of spear. A similar figure is incorporated in the frieze on the Platform of the Jaguars and Eagles.

A large altar-type platform supported by nineteen Atlantean figures stands at the rear of the upper Temple of the Warriors. This altar was originally inside the inner temple, beneath the

Two feathered-serpent columns hold up the porticoed arch to the Temple of the Warriors. Columns of the same kind are seen on other structures at Chichén Itzá.

present structure. When the superimposition was built, the altar was removed to this topmost position. Atlantean figures, holding up altars and ceremonial seats, are another kind of sculptured figure often found at Chichén Itzá. The earliest known use of Atlantean figures is on a sculpture excavated at Potrero Nuevo, Veracruz. It is of Late Preclassic date, carved approximately fifteen hundred years earlier than those here. The two largest Atlantean figures at Chichén Itzá can be seen by taking the dirt road to Old Chichén.

Steam baths are common in parts of the Maya world today. The tradition may extend back in Maya history for some two thousand years. The baths were used not only to cleanse the body but also for ritual and medical purposes. At Chichén Itzá a steam bath can be seen just a few feet from the Observatory, on the south

Detail of the serpent heads at the base of the feathered-serpent columns of the Temple of the Warriors, Chichén Itzá. Postclassic.

side of the platform. Another bath, enclosed in a bathhouse, is east of the marketplace (Mercado). This Maya bathhouse is a small, typical Puuc-style structure whose architectural design has a classic simplicity. The horizontal bands that make up the medial and cornice moldings are the only decorative elements on the building.

A short distance west of the steam bath is the Mercado. This structure may have had some purpose other than buying and selling. It may well have been the administrative center for the city. The great row of columns on a raised platform along the north side of the building is very impressive. The columns surrounding the court are the tallest at Chichén Itzá, and they must have supported a very high thatched roof. The atrium could have been used as a judicial salon. East and west of the atrium are other unrestored structures.

The Red House at Chichén Itzá rests on a very high platform. Both a flying façade and a roof comb give the building additional height. Executed in the Puuc style, this structure and many others at Chichén Itzá are Late Classic Maya.

The south part of the archaeological site is the older section of Chichén Itzá. Most of the buildings here were built by the Maya in Late Classic times; the nunnery, the Iglesia, and the Red House fall in this category. The first structure encountered on the walk to this Maya section, however, is the Temple of the High Priest (Osario), believed to be a Mexicanized Maya structure. It is easily recognized by the two great serpent heads at the top of the pyramid. These beautifully carved heads once formed part of the series of columns that supported the lintel to the temple structure. Except for the serpent heads nothing remains of the building; the rest of it tumbled down the sides of the pyramid centuries ago. The pyramid is thirty feet high and has a staircase on each of the four sides. At the top of the pyramid can be seen an open, square shaft thirty feet deep and made of cut stone. This is the entrance to a burial chamber, which is actually a natural cave. Inside, archaeologists have discovered seven tombs with their contents.

Just beyond the Osario is the Red House. The Maya name, Chichanchob, probably refers to small holes in the roof comb. The Red House is built on a platform that is unusually high for such a small structure. It is the only reconstructed building here that has a flying façade, decorated with rain-god masks, as well as a roof comb of stepped frets. Inside the three doors to the structure is a single chamber with a glyph band running the length of the east wall. From the main chamber are three additional doorways leading to inner chambers. Radiocarbon dating of the wooden lintels here and on the Iglesia gives dates of A.D. 600, 610, and 780 ± 70. Alongside the platform of the Red House is an unusual tree with brilliant orange blossoms and round leaves, called *ciricole* (a species of *Cordia* belonging to the borage family). Its leaves feel like sandpaper and have been used by the Maya over the centuries for polishing and cleansing their pottery and wooden objects.

There has always been some question about how much of the Astronomical Observatory (Caracol) had been built by the Maya before the arrival of the Mexicanized peoples from the North and the degree to which it was later altered or enlarged. A circular stairway leads to the room at the top of the circular tower. From here sightlines can be obtained for the equinoxes, the summer solstice, and the cardinal directions. The circular tower and the incensories around the Caracol platform suggest that these are later additions. The balustrade on the main stairway is in the form of a serpent, and its execution, in deep relief, is especially realistic. At the right of the main stairway to the Caracol is a small structure that was added to this platform wall toward the end of occupation here.

The Caracol commands a sweeping view of the Temple of the Wall Panels, the large palacelike structure called the Nunnery, and the Iglesia. The Temple of the Wall Panels is so named because of the glyphs (non-Maya) in a panel on the south side of the building. The Nunnery has not been completely restored, but it is obviously in the Maya Puuc style. When the right wing of this palace was dynamited by an explorer at the turn of the century, two earlier structures were revealed, one of which may date from as early as the seventh century. The Nunnery increased in size in

The Observatory, sometimes called the Caracol, at Chichén Itzá has been attributed to the Toltecs, who are believed to have dominated the site in Postclassic times. The structure

was used for astronomical calculations. In the foreground is the Temple of the Wall Panels.

*This palacelike structure, named the Nunnery by the Span-
iards, is the largest at Chichén Itzá and is Late Classic Maya.*

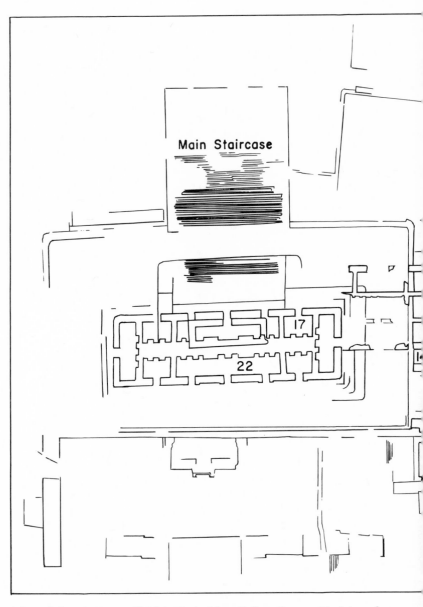

Plan of the Nunnery, Chichén Itzá. After Bolles. Rooms 22, 14, and
17 have indications of murals on the walls.

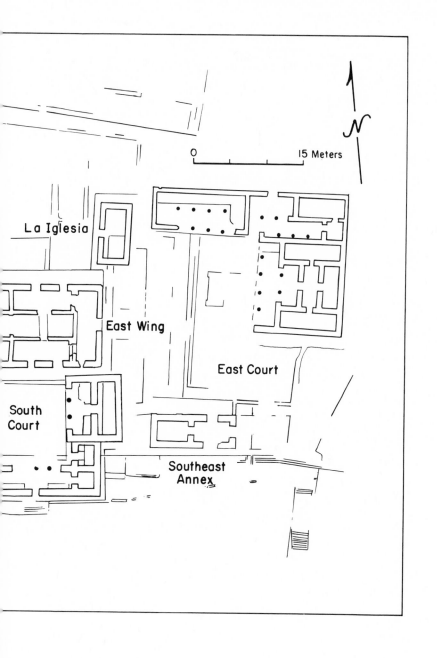

0   15 Meters

N

La Iglesia

East Wing

East Court

South
Court

Southeast
Annex

the following two centuries in seven stages of additions or renovations. The topmost structure, built of reused stones, and the present stairway are later additions. As the building stands today, it is over two hundred feet long and rises on platforms three stories above the plaza floor.

To judge from fragments of painted plaster, it is obvious that the palace structure was painted, and many of the interior rooms show signs of murals. In Room 22 on the second floor (behind the building as one goes around toward the left) are the remains of an extensive mural that at one time covered the whole room. These murals were painted on dry plaster walls in shades of red, blue, yellow, green, and pink. There are different scenes on various parts of the walls, depicting warriors with shields or throwing spears, houses with their inhabitants, and, in fragmental remains on the south wall, a sacrificial scene with nude men, some of them bound, and one with a chest wound from which blood is spurting. Fragments of murals were also found in Room 17, on the north side of the second floor, and Room 14, on the southeast side of the first floor. Little evidence of these survives today, however.

In the construction of the major sections of the palace the enlargements and changes surely reflected an increase in the power of the ruling dynasties as well as the growth of the ceremonial center and the city over a period of three hundred years. The round corners of the major platform, which now serves as a base for the second floor, are similar in style to those on the platform for the Red House. A later addition to the east wing of the Nunnery is in the Chenes style—the only structure in this style excavated to date at Chichén Itzá. The style is easily recognized by the use of mosaic-stone decoration, both above and below the medial molding, in an intricate pattern of rain-god masks. This pattern is broken above the door by an interesting panel of a seated deity in a unique circular mosaic frame.

The Iglesia, a separate, single-roomed temple adjacent to the Annex of the Nunnery, is again in the Puuc style, more commonly used by the Maya in Yucatán during Late Classic times. This small structure has above the medial molding an extremely heavy entablature composed of rain-god masks and other deities in mosaic

Adjacent to the Nunnery at Chichén Itzá is the Iglesia, a small structure that may have been a kind of temple. The high roof comb is decorated with rain-god masks. Late Classic Maya.

stone. Above this is a high roof comb decorated with three rain-god masks.

Considered one of the older Maya structures at Chichén Itzá, the Akab Dzib (Obscure Writing) is reached by taking a very short walk east of the Iglesia. This large palacelike structure has several superimpositions. The center portion is the oldest and may date from the seventh century. The north and south wings were added later, creating an impressive, massive structure, sparse in architectural detail. The south wing has a lintel with well-carved glyphs on its facing, and under the lintel is a narrative scene of a Maya lord seated on a throne. The lintel that spans this doorway gives us some idea of the importance of the structure to the Maya. The whole structure rests on a great platform, barely visible today through the vegetative growth around the structure.

From the hacienda once owned by Edward Thompson a good hike over a dust-covered trail into the bush country leads to Old Chichén (it is advisable to engage a guide for this outing). Actually, the Maya structures in this area are of the same period as that of the Nunnery, the Iglesia, and the Red House. The architecture of the buildings is consistent with the Puuc style, and they fit comfortably within the seventh-to-tenth-century time span. Alterations on some of the structures and sculptures, however, show later influence by the Mexicanized Maya. Two large Atlantean figures here support a Maya lintel dated A.D. 879, but this lintel does not belong with the Atlantean supports.

There are many buildings and sculptures to examine and investigate on this route through a hilly woodland. An early Maya door lintel, carved in stone with a plumed-serpent decoration, a house dedicated to the phallus, and a so-called hermaphroditic structure are all encountered on this trail. Nevertheless, there is only one famous building in Old Chichén, the House of the Three Lintels. This small structure, which may have been the residence of a chief and his family, is a beautiful, classic structure equaled only by the House of the Turtles at Uxmal. The building is in typical Puuc style, and the stone below the medial molding is plain. Above is an alternating pattern of rounded colonettes and lattice-frieze decoration. At each corner is the rain-god mask. Rounded engaged columns are placed at corners of the building, cut in a style identical to those on a building at Xlapak and on the Portal Vault at Labná. The House of the Three Lintels has a decorated base molding of lattice, fret, and mask design. Very few base moldings are decorated, and it is even more unusual on a building as small as this one.

Old Chichén must have been part of a larger complex associated with some of the more important structures adjacent to the Nunnery. The Late Classic architectural style of the Maya at Chichén Itzá is closely related to that of other ceremonial centers in the Northern Lowlands, such as Uxmal, Kabáh, Sayil, and Labná. At these centers we have evidence of the concerted thinking of the Maya in regard to city planning. The foreign influence in this Maya area (possibly Putun Maya) is especially notable at Chichén Itzá and in parts of Uxmal. Infiltration of these people may have begun as early as the Late Classic Period, and their presence here is evident through Postclassic times.

10   Quintana Roo: Cozumel, Tulúm, and Cobá

Cozumel

Cozumel, an island off the coast of Quintana Roo, was important in precolonial times as both a trading center and a religious shrine. It had a strategic trade location, approximately midway between seaports along the Guatemala-Honduras-Belize coast and those around the Yucatán Peninsula on the coast in Campeche and Tabasco. As a trading center and depot for merchandise, Cozumel was most active during the three centuries before the Spanish conquest. Some of the more important trade goods were cotton cloth, honey, cacao beans, jade, obsidian, quetzal plumes, and the all-important trade item, salt.

Cozumel was also important as the site of a shrine at which one could make offerings to the "Lady of the Rainbow." The shrine is believed to have stood on the north side of the island at the site of San Gervasio. It was there that the important deity Ix Chel, wife or consort of the all-embracing Maya god Itzamná, was worshiped. Ix Chel was the goddess of medicine, and pilgrims, especially prospective mothers, flocked to her shrine from near and far. Priests, hidden behind the shrine, answered the petitions to the large pottery image of the goddess. Most of the Maya temples were torn down by the Spaniards, who used the stones for their own buildings and for roads. Today there is little indication that Cozumel was once occupied by the ancient Maya.

Tulúm

Tulúm and Cobá are opposite Cozumel on the east coast of Yucatán, in the province of Quintana Roo. The mainland is dry brush country, sparsely settled, and the residents have little communication with the outside world. Approaching the rugged coast, one can see Tulúm perched high on a cliff, surrounded by a great wall, overlooking the Caribbean. Tulúm has never been given much space in literature, because it is not one of the major sites in the Yucatán Peninsula. The fame of Chichén Itzá and Uxmal has dimmed the luster of this smaller Postclassic ceremonial center.

Tulúm was first seen by Europeans when a Spanish expedition led by Juan de Grijalva sailed along the coast in the sixteenth century. In the expedition's reports describing the cities seen here at the time, one of those mentioned presumably was Tulúm. While the Spaniards exploited, placated, and decimated the population over the next few centuries, Tulúm became overgrown by dry, hostile brush vegetation. When John Lloyd Stephens and Frederick Catherwood, well known for their expeditions into Central America, arrived in 1848, they cleared and explored the ruins and exposed them to world investigation. In the twentieth century archaeological studies have been conducted by Samuel Lothrop, William Sanders, and Arthur Miller.

There are five entrances to the walled city. Through the portal arches the ruins of Tulúm, covering about sixteen acres, are spread before the visitor. One's first reaction is one of shock because of the size of the city. The buildings, especially the doorways, look as though they had been planned and built for miniature beings from another planet. The buildings resemble dollhouses clustered to form a town. The scale is even more astonishing after one has seen the great towering pyramids and palaces at Uxmal and Chichén Itzá. Nevertheless, there is something intrinsically captivating in the way the white limestone buildings are dotted within the enclosure of the great wall. Most of the buildings face west, allowing the afternoon sun to play on frescoes on the exterior façades. On the very eastern side of Tulúm the Castillo, the highest templelike building here, acts as a unifying force for the city, much as the church does today in any modern small town in Yucatán.

Many archaeological investigations have been conducted at Tulúm, including those by the Carnegie Institution of Washington and by the National Institute of Anthropology and History, in Mexico City. Tulúm and the surrounding countryside were occupied by

Aerial view of Tulúm, a Postclassic Maya city overlooking the Caribbean Sea. The perimeter of the city is outlined by a high limestone wall. The road at the upper left leads to a small landing strip.

the Maya in Preclassic times, but pottery shards constitute the only proof of that occupation. There is also evidence of occupation during the Classic era; however, the buildings one sees today are all Late Postclassic. The period is ascertained not only by the architectural style of the structures but also by the murals and the fortified walls.

The architecture shows none of the refinements of the Classic Period. For the most part it is crudely finished and lacks the proportions that would give temple and palacelike buildings distinction. Roofs are not corbled but are constructed of beams and mortar. At best the workmanship is extremely careless.

The ceremonial center, which includes some of the most important buildings at Tulúm, is separated from the rest of the city

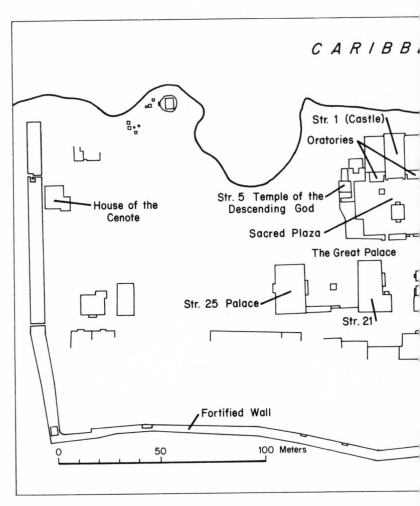

Tulúm. After Lothrop.

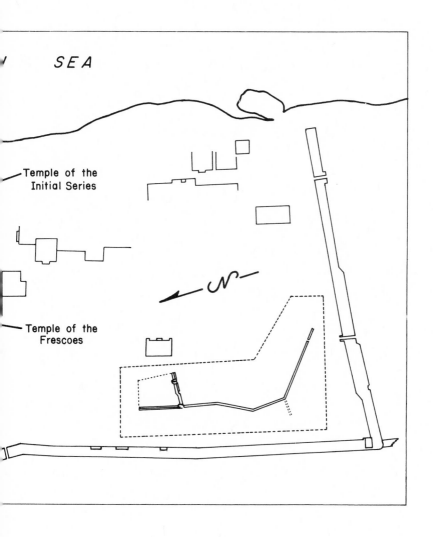

SEA

Temple of the
Initial Series

Temple of the
Frescoes

by an inner courtyard that may have been used for religious pageants and ceremonial gatherings. In this precinct are the Castillo, the Temple of the Descending God, the Temple of the Initial Series, and two small oratories. These are some of the major structures at Tulúm, on the extreme eastern side of the city. This area is closest to the sea, which serves as a backdrop for the buildings. From the Castillo the Maya had a glorious view of the rugged coastline below.

A fair-sized population lived in this rather intimately planned urban community, estimated by Michael Coe to have contained five to six hundred persons. Like most other ceremonial centers it was oriented to the cardinal points. Throughout Maya history there is religious and mythological significance to the four directions. Aside from their symbolic meanings, the cardinal directions were important factors in Maya calendrics. The times of the summer and winter solstices and the vernal and autumnal equinoxes determined the work patterns and religious events.

The most important street in the community, which separated the ceremonial center from the palace buildings, formed an axis from north to south, and many of the buildings faced this roadway. Since Tulúm was definitely planned as an urban center, parallel streets separate the various parts of the town. In this respect Tulúm is different from any other Maya site.

The fortified wall surrounding Tulúm on three sides is broken by archways that give access to other communities active during Postclassic times. Watchtowers with a single room stand on each corner of the west wall, and inside each room is an altar. At one time the exterior walls of these towers were painted with murals. Because of the protective cliff and sea there was no need for a wall on the east side of Tulúm. In contrast to the Maya Classic Period (A.D. 300-900), the Postclassic Period must have been a time of constant warfare, when ruling chiefs of small states did battle for position or territory. Walled towns were evidently necessary, and fortifications of various kinds were built for communities throughout a large part of Mesoamerica during that time. In the Maya area fortifications can be seen from Mixco Viejo, in Guatemala, to Mayapán, in Yucatán.

According to Sir J. Eric S. Thompson, Tulúm was an important trade center where merchants could route goods from the Caribbean inland to the Petén and Usumacinta regions. The town was also important for intercoastal trade. One branch of the Itzá family, the Putun Maya, notable for their aggressive conquests in other regions of Yucatán, moved into the Tulúm area from the Petén. They may have been instrumental in setting up these trade routes. Many of the Postclassic sites were along rivers and lakes or were coastal trading centers. Tulúm, as well as other coastal cities, may have had a trade alliance with Mayapán. The city was a port that could handle large seacraft on the adjacent beach.

The influences of other Mesoamerican cultures are deeply imprinted on the architecture, the decorative stucco details, and the wall murals at Tulúm. Postclassic influence is evident in the use of plumed-serpent columns on the Castillo. The talus at the foot of some of the buildings is also an imported idea, possibly from the Mayapán area.

The most important god in the sculpture at Tulúm is the "descending," or "diving," god. Niches over doorways broke the flat walls and offered a place for sculptured stucco reliefs of this god. Descending gods have been used consistently since Classic times in both Mexico and Central America. From earliest times Maya religion has embraced many heavenly deities who watch over and protect the people of this earth. The upside-down position of this deity leads one to think that it may be such a god. At El Tajín, in Veracruz, a descending god in a macabre variation becomes part of the decoration on one of the ball-court walls. In Yucatán during Late Classic times the descending god is an integral part of the mosaic design on the façade of the Palace at Sayil. And here at Tulúm, three to four hundred years later, the deity again becomes important. It is also seen at Cobá and dates from the same period. The diving-god image at these latter sites is said to be the bee god, Ah Macehcabob. Sharer, however, claims that it represents Xux Ek, the Maya "wasp star," a Venus deity. The descending god may have represented several different deities, according to the time and occasion.

Another cultural influence from the north is seen in the style

The Temple of the Frescoes is the most important building at Tulúm because of the murals under the portico. Here we see the influence of the Mixtec style. The Mixtecs were influential throughout Mesoamerica in trade, religion, and the arts. Niches over the doorways of this temple contained sculptures of seated deities and a "diving" god.

of the frescoes painted on both the interior and the exterior walls of the buildings. The best preserved of these are on the Temple of the Frescoes. Resplendent in brilliant murals of this kind, the buildings must have been impressive in their time. They would have offered a most agreeable contrast against the bleak countryside surrounding the site. The style of murals at Tulúm bears similarities to the Madrid and Paris codices. Not far down the coast from Tulúm the site of Santa Rita de Corozal also had murals on buildings in a similar style, possibly of Mixtec influence. Sylvanus G. Morley, the great Maya scholar, suggests that a new religion may have been introduced to this coast from Mexico during Late Postclassic times. If this is so, we can assume that some of the Toltec and Aztec

Section of the mural in the Temple of the Frescoes, Tulúm. This elaborate mural has been preserved because of the portico that protected the area from the weather. The style of the mural is Mixtec. Late Postclassic.

gods were assimilated into the pantheon of Mayan deities. On the other hand, the subject matter of the murals seems to be totally Maya, depicting mythological scenes. One part of the mural depicts a walking deity, possibly Ix Chel, holding two images of the rain god, Chac, and surrounded with a vegetative growth of beans and other plants.

One of the first important buildings one sees on entering the ceremonial center of Tulúm is the Temple of the Frescoes. This temple has three superimpositions, the last being a second story with a doorway that opens onto the roof. Over the door is a niche that once held a seated figure carved in stucco. Access to the second floor has been destroyed. The façade is distinctive, with four columns

311

supporting a portico—added later to enlarge the original building. By the addition of this portico the murals on the exterior walls of the original façade, dated after A.D. 1450, according to Miller, were protected from hurricanes and other storms blowing in from the Caribbean. The interior walls are also decorated with murals, and some of these are well preserved. Over the doorway of the temple are three niches in which stand stucco sculptures, rather crudely executed. The one in the center represents the descending god, and the seated sculptures at the far left and right possibly represent other deities. Separating the three sculptures are other relief panels. All are in very poor condition. Most of the structures at Tulúm have coarse medial moldings decorated with stucco and painted. On the Temple of the Frescoes the molding is decorated with rosettes, a motif used often throughout the Maya area. The façade also has two well-preserved bas-reliefs of human figures entwined in curvilinear designs.

An unusual architectural decoration on the corners of the Temple of the Frescoes is a stucco sculpture of a face mask that sweeps around the ends of the façade. In style the face is similar to a stela on the stairs of Structure 5 at El Tajín. That stela, however, was carved of stone several centuries earlier.

Tulúm was one of the last Maya ceremonial centers to use stucco as a decorative medium. There can be no comparison of the stuccoes here with the great stucco sculptures executed during the Maya Classic Period. The Temple of the Frescoes, like all other buildings at Tulúm, was plastered. Plaster hid the crude carving of the building stones and formed a base for the painted murals. Only on the outer plaster do we find murals; thus the painting must have been done just before the Conquest.

Most buildings at Tulúm have a decided outward batter that makes them look slightly top-heavy. This is especially true in the Temple of the Descending God, just north of the Castillo. In contrast to the outward batter of the exterior walls, the doorways have a noticeable inward inclination, and here again we are reminded of the style of doorways at Kabáh and other Late Classic sites in the Puuc Hills. Tulúm architects were not sensitive to the subtleties or refinements of the great Classic traditions. At Tulúm in particular

The structure called the Castillo, with its back to the sea, dominates the site of Tulúm. On each side of the staircase is a small oratory structure used by the Maya priests. The Castillo may have been a temple-type structure. However, it does have additional rooms that may have housed the priests. All the structures at Tulúm are a decadent Postclassic style.

the walls of the buildings are far from straight, the design of the buildings is clumsy, and the juxtaposition of architectural forms is awkward.

The functions of buildings at this ceremonial center seem clearer than those at other sites. Since the whole town was within a fortified wall, residences for the craftsmen and merchants had to be within the community. Farmers settled in the surrounding country may have had quick access to the city in case of attack. Fishermen may have had their own hamlets along the coast. Palace buildings may have been dwellings of the important chiefs and their families, priests, and visiting dignitaries.

Within the inner precinct of the ceremonial center the tallest and most imposing building is the Castillo. There are many super-impositions in this and other buildings at Tulúm, indicating urban growth and development. The final superimposition built on top of the Castillo had a beam-and-mortar roof. It seems obvious that the building was used as a temple and not as a "castle," as it was dubbed by the conquistadors. There was sufficient room in the structure for a priest's residence, although there is no way of knowing whether it served that purpose. A great stairway with ramps leads to the temple, three stories above ground level. Two plumed-serpent columns support the lintels of the doorways. As in the Temple of the Frescoes, niches over the doorways contain stucco sculptures, the central one again being the descending god.

On either side of the Castillo is a very small oratory building that the priests used for incantations and for making offerings. It is necessary to stoop to enter the little door to this single-chambered structure.

Just north of the Castillo is Structure 5, usually called the Temple of the Descending, or Diving, God. The design of this miniature temple follows that of other structures here. The vertical walls are decidedly battered, a cornice encircles the temple top, a descending god is carved in stucco over the doorway, and the walls were plastered and painted with frescoes, few traces of which remain today.

Perhaps the most finely executed and best-preserved sculpture of a descending god at Tulúm is that on Structure 25, just north of the Temple of the Frescoes. The interlaced decorative detail on the sides of the god is especially noteworthy, and some of the original color is still visible on the deity. Structures 25 and 21 are the largest palacelike buildings at Tulúm.

Southeast of the inner precinct is the Temple of the Initial Series. This building originally housed a stela, found broken into pieces, that had a date corresponding to A.D. 564. Since this is a date of the Initial Series calculation, the structure was named from the stela. (The Initial Series, or Long Count, is the name of the Maya system for recording time. The initial starting date for the Maya calendar is the year 3114 B.C., possibly a mythological creation date.) Knowing that the building was constructed many centuries after this date, one can only guess that the stela was moved to Tulúm from some other ceremonial center. The stela is now housed in the British Museum. The Temple of the Initial Series, as well as some other buildings at Tulúm, has walls punctuated by open windows. At one time the Temple of the Initial Series had a stucco façade, but little remains today to indicate the content or quality.

If there is time at Tulúm to investigate a building outside the great wall, a hike some distance north will lead to Structure 59. This edifice is unique at Tulúm in having the only roof comb. The design of the roof comb is that of open triangles arranged in a double row.

A pathway north of the Temple of the Descending God leads down the embankment to the sea. Today, as in the time when Tulúm was active, fishermen easily gather a plentiful catch of fish, lobsters, conches, and clams. The view along the coast is highlighted by rock outcroppings, stretches of white-sand beaches, and the blue-green sea splashing against large rocks that have tumbled from the cliff into the water.

Tulúm lacks the refinement, beauty, and creative ingenuity of the work of earlier Maya craftsmen. Nevertheless, there is a charm about it. The site imparts a sense of struggle and accomplishment. There is much to explore, to investigate, and to search for in the diminutive style of the architecture, which is distinct from that of other Maya sites. The beauty and charm of the spot are not easily forgotten. As in ancient times, Tulúm stands today as a solitary buttress against the sea.

Cobá

Travelers wishing to see the archaeological ruins of Quintano Roo will find that they can visit both Tulúm and Cobá in the same day, for these two ancient urban centers are not far apart. Cobá has a much earlier history, starting in the Preclassic Period and continuing through the Late Postclassic Period. Its major construc-

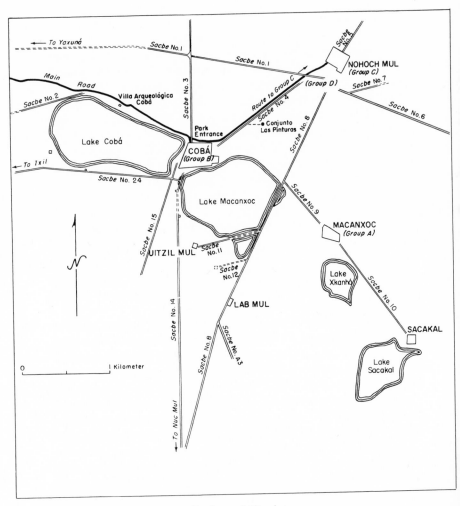

Cobá. After Thompson, Pollock, and Charlot.

tion was in the Middle Classic Period, and most of the monuments have dates in the seventh and eighth centuries.

The earliest known monument is dated A.D. 623. Cobá, once a large city, came to an end much earlier than did other Classic Maya cities in the Northern Lowlands. Both Cobá and Edzna show influence from the Maya Southern Lowlands, and most likely both were involved in a trade network or maintained depots for such produce as salt, cotton, and seafoods. After the city was abandoned, it was reoccupied in Late Postclassic times when Tulúm was important as a coastal trading port. At this later time the two cities share similar features in their decadent architectural style, also seen at Mayapán, in which the descending god was popularly used on the façades of temple buildings.

Archaeological investigations were first undertaken at Cobá by J. P. Contreras and D. Elizalde in 1886. They were followed by Theobert Maler in 1891, by Thomas Gann in 1926, and by Sir J. Eric S. Thompson, Harry E. D. Pollock, and Jean Charlot from 1926 to 1930, when the Carnegie Institute had the area surveyed and the various monuments recorded.

Cobá, meaning "water stirred by the wind," has not been excavated to any degree. Most of the city and the many *sacbeob* (causeways) still lie buried in the heavy jungle undergrowth. Cobá reached the status of a regional capital in the eighth century and had an estimated population of 55,000. Its total extent is unknown, but it may well have controlled the area from the Caribbean to Yaxuná, only a few miles from Chichén Itzá. During the eighth century Uxmal, Edzna, and Puuc Chichén Itzá may well have been regional capitals. Because of the series of five freshwater lakes in the area, settlers were attracted to this particular region at a very early time, and by Middle Classic times it was one of the largest Maya cities in the Northern Lowlands.

Evidence of Cobá's importance is its *sacbé*, the longest known in the Maya world, over sixty miles long and extending to Yaxuná. This is a major causeway, and it must have been extremely important for utilitarian and military purposes as well as for pageantry. The most recent survey of the *sacbeob* at Cobá (Folan, Kintz, and Fletcher) shows that more than fifty have been found, all radiating from the center of the city and dividing it into four major sections. Aside from the Yaxuná *sacbé* there is another fairly long *sacbé* to the village of Ixil. Both Yaxuná and Ixil could well have been under the sovereignty of Cobá, the regional capital. All the *sacbeob* are very straight and well constructed, often passing through swamps, lakes and other varied terrain. Constructed of inner and outer retaining walls with an inner core filled with stone, these roadways were solidified with lime and then plastered to provide a smooth surface. The width varied from approximately nine feet to sixty feet (where there were plazas), and the height from one to three feet. One *sacbé* rose twenty-one feet above ground level; the height varied according to the terrain.

Ramps were sometimes used at large intersections or at important civic complexes. Other ramps were designed to accommodate the irregularities in the terrain. Culverts were used on *sacbeob* in wet areas. Some *sacbeob* had defensive walls at intervals. On the sides of these roadways can be seen the open quarries mined for their construction. Other quarries were in closed mines reached by tunnels. Folan, Kintz, and Fletcher report that one mine had thirty-one hourglass-shaped supports inside a major chamber. We can imagine a large corvée labor force being mustered when major construction was needed. No doubt many of the workers were slaves captured in warfare; slaves were an important trade item to the Maya. Some quarries go back to Early Classic, and it is believed that Lake Macanxoc, near Cobá, was formed by such a quarry.

Dikes and check dams are noted throughout the city, as well as cenotes, wells, and chaltunes, indicating the extent of water resources. The surrounding land has been altered for hydraulic control and urban development.

A significant trade route from the coastal region of Tulúm and other eastern seaboard towns must have passed through Cobá to Yaxuná and then on to Chichén Itzá. The center for trade, the markets, and control of the trade routes could have been at Cobá. Obsidian, flint, and other hard stones from the central and southern Maya areas were traded for salt, cotton, honey, and other important commodities from the northern coastal areas.

The city with its many large ceremonial complexes covers a

large area. The major groups of buildings are those at Nohoch Mul (Group C), Cobá (Group B), and Macanxoc (Group A). Sacakal and many other smaller complexes away from Cobá's central axis cover several square miles. The central area of the city has clusters of palaces, plazas, and religious structures. Residential areas are in groupings surrounding the five lakes. Footpaths through the jungle lead to the many stelae and other monuments that dot the complexes. Mounds associated with the stelae are probably temples or civic structures still to be uncovered.

At Cobá there are more than thirty-two stelae, twenty-three of which are sculptured; most of these were carved during the Middle Classic Period. The limestone used in this area for carving is of a very poor quality and often erodes in flakes from exposure to the weather. The style of the carving and the theme of the reliefs show the influence of the Petén. Sir J. Eric S. Thompson believed that many of the monuments at Group B were reset in shrinelike areas at a later time, even centuries after they were originally erected. The stela found at Tulúm, now in the British Museum, may have come from Cobá, since it is Classic Period and Tulum is Late Postclassic. The shrines of Cobá show no indication of roofs, but they may have been made of perishable materials. In contrast, the monuments at Group C (Nohoch Mul) seem to be in their original position, and they are placed in association with important structures. A walk along foot trails through the bushy undergrowth gives the traveler a chance to see the many causeways, stelae, and altars. A competent guide is essential, and one is sometimes available at the caretaker's house, where guests must register.

The two major pyramids at Cobá are the Castillo (Structure 1 in Group C) at Nohoch Mul facing Lake Macanxoc, and the Castillo, also known as the Iglesia, between Lake Cobá and Lake Macanxoc at Cobá (Group B). Both pyramids are approximately eighty feet high and were constructed in the Middle of the Classic Period. The pyramids at Group B and C resemble one another. Both have inset, rounded corners at the front. The pyramid in Group B has the same inset corners at the rear, but the rear corners of the Nohoch Mul pyramid have plain, rounded ends. (Inset corners were also used at Tikál, but they are squared instead of

There are two major pyramids at Cobá. This pyramid is at Nohoch Mul. The foundation is Late Classic, but the structure on its top is Postclassic and in many ways resembles the structures at Tulúm and Mayapán.

rounded.) The Cobá (Group B) Iglesia pyramid has nine terraces, whereas at Nohoch Mul there are only seven. Both temples are Postclassic. At one time all these structures were painted in polychrome. Under a stela in the Iglesia temple was found an offering consisting of a mother-of-pearl pendant and a jade figurine of the merchant god Ek Chuah. The base of the Nohoch Mul pyramid, 180 by 198 feet, is the largest of the entire area. Under the floor of this temple was found an offering of jade beads, shell pectorals, and coral beads, all placed in a container. These two major groups, Nohoch Mul and the Iglesia at Cobá, Group B, are approximately one mile apart. Many of the structures around these two pyramids, as well as the bases of the pyramids, are from Classic times, but

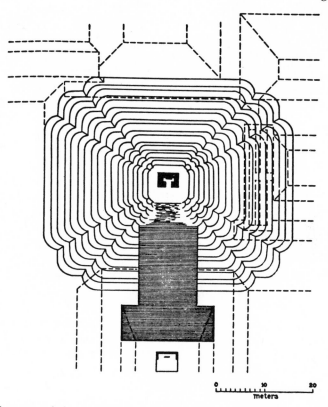

A drawing of the Castillo (Group B), Cobá, with its inset rounded corners and the grand staircase. After Thompson, Pollock, and Charlot.

the temple structures on their summit are Postclassic, built during a much later occupation, just before the Spanish Conquest.

The largest and most compact ceremonial center at Cobá is Group B. The scheme of the architectural structures and courts bears similarities to that of centers in the Petén. Group B is oriented to the cardinal points, as are most other Northern Lowland sites, and the main pyramid faces west. The one ball court found here

321

so far is also close in design to the ball courts of the Petén and Copán. In Group D (near Nohoch Mul) another ball court with the same kind of design has been found, and it is likely that there are many more in a city of this size. Ball-court rings found in Group B at Cobá come as a surprise, because we do not usually associate them with the Classic Petén tradition.

At Group C (Nohoch Mul) the ceremonial center is smaller and less compact than the center at Group B. The complex rests on a slight rise of the terrain. There are indications of multiple-storied buildings in this area, not unusual for Classic Maya cities. The view from the top of the Nohoch Mul Pyramid shows the flatness of the barren landscape, the radiant lakes shimmering in the dazzling sun, and the vastness of the junglelike countryside extending to the very edge of the distant horizon.

In front of the great pyramid at Nohoch Mul is a plaza area covering several acres. Here, as in other sections of Cobá, the buildings (see Structure 1) had both stone corbeled vaults and unvaulted roofs in Classic times. On one side of this plaza is Structure X, a partly restored, palacelike building with two rooms. In front of Structure X is Stela 20, the best-preserved stela at the site, depicting one of the great Maya lords holding a ceremonial bar and standing on two dwarflike figures. On either side of the main personage are kneeling figures. Glyphs indicate the date, corresponding to A.D. 780. Looking from the great pyramid at Nohoch Mul, one can see in the distant jungle a cone-shaped unexcavated structure called El Cono (in Maya, Xaibe).

A short walk south of Nohoch Mul will take one to a complex that has a pyramid temple known as the Conjunto Las Pinturas, built in Postclassic times. This structure, like all the others at Cobá, is carved of limestone. The main doorway of the temple faces north, and the lintel is supported by a single column. In a panel above the doorway is a painted mural, with much of the original color, that gives the building its name. The style here is similar to that of the Temple of the Frescoes at Tulúm and is in the tradition of the paintings in the Mixtec and Aztec codices. The single-vaulted chamber to this temple has four doorways. From the inside of the temple a remarkable view through the east doorway reveals the

Nohoch Mul pyramid rising above the distant vegetation. The platform for the temple has two altars. At the base of the Conjunto Las Pinturas are the foundations of several structures, possibly shrines, that were added to the small plaza at a much later time. Here too can be seen fragments of stelae, altars, and a stone phallus.

Group A at Macanxoc, a small ceremonial center south of Conjunto Las Pinturas, is partway between Lake Macanxoc and Lake Xkanha on *Sacbé* No. 9. No excavation has been done here, but several stelae and altars, all from the Middle Classic Period, can be seen. The focal point of Group A is a small pyramid in poor condition, approximately forty feet high. Beyond the major lake area are structures scattered into the far distance, none of which have been excavated.

Suggestions for Reaching Archaeological Zones

Pacific Slope: By private car. A knowledgeable guide from Guatemala City who is familiar with the fincas around El Baúl and La Democracia would be advisable.

Iximché and Zaculeu: Both of these sites can be reached by car from Guatemala City. For Iximché take the highway going toward Lake Atitlán and turn off for the village called Tecpan. Since the road is bad from this village to the ruins, a local bus can be used for the last two-mile drive. For Zaculeu continue to Quetzaltenango and then proceed to Huehuetenango. Hotel accommodations are available in both these communities. The drive from Huehuetenango to the Zaculeu ruins is only two miles. At Zaculeu there is also a small landing field for private aircraft.

Mixco Viejo: By car from Guatemala City. Be sure to check the conditions of the river crossing on this side of Mixco Viejo. Sometimes the little bridge is washed out. Should the river be impassable by car, the walk from the river to the ruins is approximately two miles.

Quiriguá: By car from Guatemala City. The trip can be made in one day. There are no accommodations.

Copán: From Guatemala City it is possible to charter a private plane for Copán, but it is expensive. Occasionally planes are scheduled from Tegucigalpa, in Honduras. A travel agent in Guatemala City may be of assistance in this kind of arrangement. It is also possible to fly to San Pedro Sula, in Honduras, from Guatemala City. From there one can hire a car or take a local bus over the long, dusty road to San José de Copán. Another alternative is to take the highway from Guatemala City to Puerto Barrios. At Río Honda leave the highway and proceed south to Chiquimula. Continue a little farther south to the intersection. At this point change routes to a secondary road (21) and continue toward Jocatan. This road leads to the border crossing and continues to Copán. Sometimes there is difficulty in crossing the border on a Sunday. The ruins are only a mile from Copán village. Modest accommodations are available in the village.

Seibal: By plane from Guatemala City to Flores. At this point a four-wheel-drive vehicle is needed for the trip on the dirt road to Sayaxché and Seibal. It is necessary to cross the Pasión River on a ferry this side of Sayaxché. From Sayaxché the trip up the Pasión River is made by dugout canoe if the road is in poor condition, especially during the rainy season, or by vehicle if the condition of the rutted road to Seibal is satisfactory.

Tikal: By plane from Guatemala City to Tikal. During the rainy season flights can be irregular. A network of dirt roads connects Belize with Flores, Guatemala; San Pedro Sula, Honduras; and Tikal. The roads are not always passable because of the rains. If one takes a flight from Guatemala City to Flores, better accommodations will be available, and a more reliable schedule can be planned. Flores can then be used as a headquarters for trips by bus to Tikal and to Seibal. Meager accommodations are available in Tikal.

Tulúm: A small landing field one mile from Tulúm is available for private planes from Mérida, Mexico, or Cozumel. It is possible to go by boat from Cozumel to Tulúm, but weather conditions often make the trip impossible or inadvisable. A highway is now open from Mérida to Puerto Juárez, and it continues along the Caribbean coast to Tulúm. This trip can be made by private car, and there are accommodations at Tancah, just north of Tulúm, or at Cobá.

Cobá: The site is easily reached by the same highway that goes to Tulúm. Accommodations are available at Villa Arqueológica Cobá, overlooking Lake Cobá.

Chichén Itzá, Uxmal, and Kabáh: These sites can easily be reached by car from Mérida, and accommodations are available.

Sayil, Xlapak, and Labná: By car from Mérida or Kabáh. A new hard-surface road, starting five miles south of Kabáh, goes to Sayil, Xlapak, and Labná.

Palenque: By scheduled airline from Mexico City or Mérida to

Villahermosa. Transportation by car from Villahermosa to Palenque can be arranged. The drive is seventy miles. Modest accommodations are available in Palenque.

Edzna: An hour's drive by car on the highway from Campeche to Chencoyi starts the journey to Edzna. Continue approximately twenty miles beyond Chencoyi for the turn south to Edzna.

Yaxchilán and Bonampak: The easiest way to get to these remote sites is by private local aircraft from Villahermosa or Palenque. The trip is made to both sites in the same day. There are no accommodations at either site. These sites can also be reached from Sayaxché by dugout canoe along the Usumacinta River if advance arrangements have been made to be picked up by a Palenque plane, or if arrangements have been made to be picked up on the Mexican side of the Usumacinta, from which in good weather it is possible to drive to Palenque.

Organized Tours

Organized tours to some of the archaeological ruins are available. These include Uxmal, Kabáh, Labná, Sayil, Xlapak, and Chichén Itzá, in Yucatán. In Guatemala organized tours go to Tikal. The other ruins require private car, plane, or train transportation "on your own." Local travel agencies in the Maya area can be especially helpful in arranging transportation with drivers. Arrangements also need to be made for competent guides.

A Word About Weather and Clothing

Persons traveling to the Maya ruins should dress as casually and travel as light as possible. Slacks for both men and women are essential for most areas. To avoid sunburn and, in a few places, insects, it is best to keep the arms and legs covered and wear a hat with a brim to shade the face. The tropical sun can give a very bad burn. Be sure to include sunglasses and suntan lotion. Sneakers or rubber-soled shoes with low heels are a must.

A Word About Weather and Clothing

In the Guatemalan highlands, while visiting the sites of Zaculeu, Iximché, and Mixco Viejo, one should be prepared for cooler weather. Altitudes range from 4,500 to 6,500 feet, and evenings can be chilly. A sweater or jacket can come in handy. At Copán, even though the altitude is only 2,000 feet, there are occasionally chilly nights. The tropical lowlands are hot and humid. For Tikal, Seibal, Palenque, Quiriguá, Bonampak, and Yaxchilán, clothing should be light and washable. Shorts are not recommended here because of insects and the danger of sunburn. Those who are allergic to insect bites should carry insect repellent. Swimming pools are available at most of the larger hotels.

In Yucatán and Quintana Roo it is always hot, though drier than in the tropical lowlands. Nights are somewhat cooler. Again, light clothing is essential. Dinner dress at hotels is extremely casual. Dresses for women or jackets and ties for men are unnecessary.

Laundry service is not available at most outlying places. It is available in Guatemala City. Bathing suits will come in handy for those who enjoy swimming, since pools are available at Uxmal, Chichén Itzá, Guatemala City, Villahermosa, and Campeche.

During the rainy season, from May to December, a plastic raincoat is needed. In Yucatán the rainy season has many sunny days, and when rain does come, it is often a short shower followed by sunny skies. In the tropical lowlands in the Petén and along the Usumacinta and Motagua rivers, however, rain is more frequent. The best time to visit the Maya area is from January to April, although travelers make the trip throughout the summer and fall.

Selected Readings

Adams, Richard, E. E., ed. *The Origins of Maya Civilization.* Albuquerque, N.Mex., 1977.

Benson, Elizabeth P. *The Maya World.* New York, 1967.

————. *The Sea in the Pre-Columbian World.* Washington, D.C., 1977.

Coe, Michael D. *The Maya.* Rev. ed. New York, 1980.

Coe, William R. *Tikal: A Handbook of the Ancient Maya Ruins.* Philadelphia, 1967.

Culbert, T. Patrick, ed. *The Classic Maya Collapse.* Albuquerque, N.Mex., 1973.

Folan, W. J., E. Kintz, and L. Fletcher. *Cobá, a Classic Maya Metropolis.* New York, 1983.

Gallenkamp, Charles. *Maya.* 3d ed. New York, 1985.

Greene, Merle. *Ancient Maya Relief Sculpture.* New York, 1967.

————. *Maya Sculpture.* Berkeley, Calif., 1972.

Hammond, Norman, ed. *Mesoamerican Archaeology: New Approaches.* Austin, Tex., 1974.

Henderson, John S. *The World of the Ancient Maya.* Ithaca, N.Y., 1981.

Kidder, Alfred V., Jesse L. Jennings, and Edwin M. Shook. *Excavations at Kaminaljuyú, Guatemala.* Carnegie Institution of Washington Publication No. 561. Washington, D.C., 1946.

Kubler, George. *The Art and Architecture of Ancient America.* Baltimore, Md., 1962.

Longyear, John M. *Copán Ceramics.* Carnegie Institution of Washington Publication No. 597. Washington, D.C., 1952.

Lothrop, Samuel K. *Tulúm: An Archaeological Study of the East Coast of Yucatán.* Carnegie Institution of Washington Publication No. 335. Washington, D.C., 1924.

————, et al. *Essays in Pre-Columbian Art and Archaeology.* Cambridge, Mass., 1964.

Marcus, Joyce. *Emblem and State in the Classic Maya Lowlands.* Washington, D.C., 1976.

Maudslay, Alfred P. *Archaeology. Biologia Centrali-Americana: Or, Contributions to the Knowledge of the Fauna and Flora of Central*

America. 5 vols. London, 1889-1902. Reissue. Ed. by F. Ducane Godman and Osbert Salvin. 4 vols. Norman, Okla., 1983.

Morley, Sylvanus G. *The Ancient Maya.* 4th ed. Revised by Robert J. Sharer. Stanford, 1983.

———. *The Inscriptions of Petén.* Carnegie Institution of Washington Publication No. 435. 5 vols. Washington, D.C., 1937-38.

Proskouriakoff, Tatiana. *An Album of Maya Architecture.* Carnegie Institution of Washington Publication No. 558. Washington, D.C., 1946. Reprint. Norman, Okla., 1963.

Recinos, Adrián. *Popol Vuh: The Sacred Book of the Ancient Quiché Maya.* Norman, Okla., 1950.

Robiscek, Francis. *Copán: Home of the Maya Gods.* New York, 1972.

Ruppert, Karl, J. Eric S. Thompson, and Tatiana Proskouriakoff. *Bonampak, Chiapas, Mexico.* Carnegie Institution of Washington Publication No. 602. Washington, D.C., 1955.

Ruz Lhuillier, Alberto. *The Civilization of the Ancient Maya.* Mexico City, 1970.

Smith, A. Ledyard, and Alfred V. Kidder. *Excavations at Nebaj, Guatemala.* Carnegie Institution of Washington Publication No. 594. Washington, D.C., 1951.

Spinden, Herbert J. *A Study of Maya Art.* Memoirs of the Peabody Museum of Archaeology and Ethnology, Harvard University. Vol. 6. Cambridge, Mass., 1913.

Stephens, John Lloyd. *Incidents of Travel in Central America, Chiapas, and Yucatan.* New York, 1841.

———. *Incidents of Travel in Yucatán.* New York, 1843. Reprint. Norman, Okla., 1962.

Stone, Doris. *Pre-Columbian Man Finds Central America.* Cambridge, Mass., 1972.

Thompson, J. Eric S. *The Rise and Fall of Maya Civilization.* Norman, Okla., 1954; 2d ed., enlarged, 1966.

———. *Maya Hieroglyphic Writing.* Norman, Okla., 1960.

———. *Maya History and Religion.* Norman, Okla., 1970.

———, H. E. D. Pollock, and J. Charlot. *A Preliminary Study of the Ruins of Cobá, Quintana Roo, Mexico.* Carnegie Institution of Washington Publication No. 424. Washington, D.C., 1932.

Wauchope, Robert, gen. ed. *Handbook of Middle American Indians.* Vols. 2, 3. Austin, Tex., 1965.

Woodbury, Richard B., and Aubrey Trik. *The Ruins of Zacaleu, Guatemala.* Boston, 1953.

Index

A

Abaj Takalik, Guatemala: 27, 30, 32, 118; monuments, 32, 37
Acancéh, Mexico: 274
Accommodations: 324-26
Acropolis, Tikal: 17, 51
Adobe: 188-89, 192, 212
Agriculture: 50-51
Aguateca, Guatemala: 72, 174
Ah Cacan (Tikal aristocrat): 60, 62
Ah Cacau (ruler): 10, 55, 57, 68, 72
Ah Macehcabob (god): 309
Ahpo-Hel (mother of Kan Xul): 153
Ah Puch (god): 25
Akab Dzib, Chichén Itza: 301
Altar de Sacrificios, Guatemala: 4, 13, 174, 175; architecture, 177; pottery, 177
Altars: 32, 104, 107; Tikal, 51, 55, 69, 72; Copán, 75, 77, 85, 88-89, 100, 101-104; Quiriguá, 117, 119; Olmec, 118; Palenque, 142; Yaxchilán, 155, 158, 163; Seibal, 180, 182; Chichén Itzá, 289-90; Tulúm, 308; Cobá, 323; see also monuments, stelae
Altun Ha, Belize: 23
Alvarado, Pedro de: 192-93, 202
American Indians: 89
Ancestor worship: 4

Andesite: 83
Andrews, A. P.: 13
Andrews, George F.: 266
Annals of the Cakchiquels: 25
Aqueducts: 151
Archaeology Museum, Guatemala City: 72
Archaic Period: 3
Architecture: 9, 17-18, 21, 22, 24, passim; Tikal, 48, 51; Quiriguá, 121-22; Palenque, 158; Piedras Negras, 158; Yaxchilán, 158; Altar de Sacrificios, 177; Seibal, 177; Kaminaljuyú, 189; Zaculeu, 193-96; Toltec, 202; Aztec, 202, 204; Chichén Itzá, 217; Dzibilchaltún, 217; Uxmal, 217, 222-23; see also monuments, sculpture, stelae
Arroyo Yaxchilán: 154
Artifacts, theft of: 39
Astrology: 77, 107, 287; see also astronomy
Astronomical Observatory (Caracol), Chichén Itzá: 293
Astronomy: 7, 9, 19, 23, 24, 77, 110, 132, 220, 224; see also astrology
Asunción Mita, Guatemala: 98
Aztec: 12, 40, 96, 214, 276, 282, 287, 288, 289; influence on Mayas, 7; architecture, 202, 204; oppression of Mayas, 208; gods, 310-

11; codices, 322

B

Ball, Joseph: 275
Ball courts: 75, 77, 151-52, 309; Tikal, 60; Copán, 96, 100, 121, 322; Quiriguá, 121; Yaxchilán, 160; Seibal, 180; Kaminaljuyú, 188; Zaculeu, 196; Mixco Viejo, 204-206; Iximché, 209, 212-13; Uxmal, 232, 233; Chichén Itzá, 279, 282; Cobá, 321-22; Petén, 322
Ball game: 37, 39, 77, 96, 98, 189, 279, 282
Bat Palace: see Palace of Windows, Tikal
Beards: 89-90, 114
Becan, Mexico: 4, 266
Bee Ruin: 172
Belize: 4, 8, 9, 16, 123, 217, 303, 325
Belize River: 128
Berlin, Heinrich: 14
Bernoulli, Gustav: 44
Bilbao, Guatemala: 27, 37-40
Bilbao (Parsons): 39
Bird Jaguar (ruler): 10
Blom, Franz: 129
Bolivia: 151
Bonampak, Mexico: 55, 77, 164-73, 326, 327; frescoes, 9; murals, 23, 104, 172-73; influence of Yaxchilán, 163-64; ceremonial center, 164; ally of Yaxchilán, 165,

monuments, palaces,
temples
Stephens, John Lloyd: 89,
112, 129, 304
Stormy Sky (ruler): 10,
49, 72
Stromsvik, Gustav: 112
Structure 1, Bonampak:
164, 171-72
Structure 3, Bonampak:
171
Structure 33, Yaxchilán:
160-61, 163
Structure 79, Seibal:
186-87
Stucco: 133, 150, 172,
182, 274, 312
Sun-at-Horizon (ruler): 11
Sun disks: 37
Superimpositions: 24, 50,
51, 119, 194-96, 206,
212, 222-23, 225,
289-90, 301, 314
Swidden: *see* slash-and-
burn agriculture

T

Tabasco, Mexico: 9, 13,
16, 28, 123, 275, 303
Tablet of the Palace,
Palenque: 142, 153
Tablets: 150; Palenque,
142, 153
Talud-tablero: 274
Tancah, Mexico: 325
Tararindito, Guatemala:
174
Tarascans: 40
Tecpán, Guatemala: 209,
213, 324
Tegucigalpa, Honduras:
324
Tehuantepec (isthmus):
30
Temple IV, Tikal: 48
Temple V, Tikal: 51
Temple VI, Tikal: *see*
Temple of the Inscrip-
tions, Tikal
Temple 22, Copán: 107
Temple of the Count,
Palenque: 152-53

Temple of the Cross,
Palenque: 150-51
Temple of the Descending
God, Tulúm: 314
Temple of the Frescoes,
Tulúm: 310-12, 314,
322
Temple of the High
Priest, Chichén Itzá:
292
Temple of the Initial
Series, Tulúm: 314-15
Temple of the Inscrip-
tions, Copán: 104
Temple of the Inscriptions,
Palenque: 21, 23, 55,
129, 132, 141-44, 150
Temple of the Inscriptions
(Temple VI), Tikal: 55,
68
Temple of the Jaguar
Priest, Tikal: 62
Temple of the Jaguars,
Chichén Itzá: 276, 282
Temple of the Sun,
Palenque: 150
Temple of the Wall
Panels, Chichén Itzá:
293
Temple of the Warriors,
Chichén Itzá: 287-90
Temples: 9, 16-17, 21,
22, 24, 26, 44, 48, 51,
57, 74, 104, 107,
passim; of Palenque,
21, 23, 55, 129, 132,
141-44, 150-53; Tikal,
44, 48, 55, 62, 68, 180,
278; Copán, 98, 100;
Quiriguá, 113; Seibal,
180, 182; Uaxactún,
180; Zaculeu, 194-95;
Mixco Viejo, 204;
Iximché, 214; Uxmal,
222-24, 237, 241;
Kabah, 249, 252-53;
Edzna, 267, 270-71;
Chichén Itzá, 277-78,
282, 287-90; Cobá,
319, 320; *see also*
architecture, monu-
ments, palaces, pyra-
mids, stelae
Tenochtitlán, Mexico: 287

Teotihuacán, Mexico: 7-8,
13, 37, 41, 49, 67, 68,
189, 274-76; demise,
50
Terminal Classic Period:
13, 74, 175, 180, 208,
217, 246, 248, 274-76,
289
Terracing: 50
Theft of artifacts: 39
Thompson, Edward: 129,
278, 301
Thompson, Sir J. Eric S.:
12, 150, 172, 275, 309,
317, 319
Tierra del Fuego, Chile: 3
Tikal, Guatemala: 4,
9-11, 13, 14, 17, 19,
23, 24, 41-74, 114,
142, 189, 200, 274,
325-27; ceremonial
center, 41, 44, 48, 51,
57, 67, 68, 72, 74;
Museum, 41, 62;
Central Acropolis, 44,
62, 67; excavations, 44,
48; North Acropolis,
44, 48, 49, 51, 55;
pyramids, 44, 51, 320;
social structure, 44;
temples, 44, 48, 57,
60, 62, 180, 278;
architecture, 48, 51;
as necropolis, 48-50;
Palace, 48; burials, 49,
55, 60, 73; emblem
glyphs, 51, 72, 84;
Great Plaza, 51, 62, 67;
agriculture, 50-51;
Acropolis, 51; altars,
51, 55, 69, 72; plazas,
51; roof combs, 51;
stelae, 51, 55; sculp-
ture, 55, 60-62; Temple
of the Inscriptions, 55,
68; monuments, 57,
100; Temple I, 57, 60,
62; Temple II, 57, 62;
ball courts, 60; Plaza of
the Seven Temples, 60;
carved lintels, 62;
Temple III, 62; Temple
IV, 62; Temple of the
Jaguar Priest, 62; aris-